MISSION DRIFT

THE UNSPOKEN CRISIS FACING
LEADERS, CHARITIES, AND CHURCHES

PETER GREER // CHRIS HORST

FOREWORD BY ANDY CROUCH

BETHANY HOUSE PUBLISHERS

a division of Baker Publishing Group
Minneapolis, Minnesota

© 2014 by Peter Greer and Chris Horst

Published by Bethany House Publishers
11400 Hampshire Avenue South
Bloomington, Minnesota 55438
www.bethanyhouse.com

Bethany House Publishers is a division of
Baker Publishing Group, Grand Rapids, Michigan

Paperback edition published 2015
ISBN 978-0-7642-1164-5

Printed in the United States of America

The Library of Congress has cataloged the original edition as follows:
Greer, Peter
    Mission drift : the unspoken crisis facing leaders, charities, and churches / Peter Greer and Chris Horst, with Anna Haggard.
        pages cm
    Includes bibliographical references.
    Summary: "The CEO of HOPE International shows organizations how to stay true to their Christian mission, and offers tools for getting back on track if 'drifting'"— Provided by publisher.
    ISBN 978-0-7642-1101-0 (cloth : alk. paper) 1. Mission of the church. I. Title.
    BV601.8.G74 2014
    267'.1—dc23   2013039136

Cover design by Lookout Design, Inc.

Authors are represented by Wolgemuth & Associates.

17   18   19   20   21   22   23   9   8   7   6   5   4   3

"Peter Greer and Chris Horst have identified one of the deepest challenges any leader faces: how to ensure that an organization stays true to its mission, especially when that mission becomes countercultural."

—from the foreword by Andy Crouch, executive editor, *Christianity Today*

"During my years as a CEO—first in the for-profit sector and later in the nonprofit sector—I've always found it a challenge to stay on mission. Many of us in leadership have learned—often painfully—that our mission needs to be built into every aspect of our organization, from leadership to receptionist, from hiring to implementation. We can't afford not to follow the lessons in this valuable book."

—Richard Stearns, president, World Vision U.S. and author,
Unfinished: Believing Is Only the Beginning

"Keeping an eternal perspective is essential in our work. *Mission Drift* gives a clear message inspiring and challenging us to intentionally keep Christ at the center of all efforts. As Paul commands us, 'Whatever you do, whether in word or deed, do it all in the name of the Lord Jesus.'"

—David Green, founder & CEO, Hobby Lobby Stores, Inc.

"Essential reading for twenty-first-century believers if we are to gain new vision, unity, and strength. *Mission Drift* is spine straightening, mind clearing, and courage inspiring. This book is true-north wisdom for leaders—and a gift of hope for the world God loves."

—Kelly Monroe Kullberg, founder, The Veritas Forum and author,
Finding God Beyond Harvard: The Quest for Veritas

"Paying attention is often harder than it seems. Perhaps nowhere is this any more important than in acts of Christian leadership. As this book makes clear, the possibilities of drift are many and substantial. Those charged with leadership face diversions from many directions. To pay careful, humble, and relentless attention to the heart of our Christian mission is an essential part of faithful leadership. Read this book and be helped in doing so!"

—Mark Labberton, president, Fuller Theological Seminary

"Every organization has to guard against losing or even abandoning its original purpose. But the problem is especially acute in Christian organizations because Christianity is increasingly becoming countercultural. When the entire culture drifts in a bad direction, simple inertia can pull a Christian mission off course, even if no one really intends it. Thank God for Peter Greer and Chris Horst for having the courage to identify this growing crisis. They do a magnificent job, not only of diagnosing the problem, but of giving sound and practical advice on how to prevent your ministry from becoming a hostage of a hostile culture. If you want to prevent that in your own organization, you should read this book."

—Jay W. Richards, PhD, author, *Money, Greed, and God* and *New York Times* bestsellers *Infiltrated* and *Indivisible*

"We Christians are amazing at putting our passions into action with an entrepreneurial spirit. Yet we have a terrible track record of sustaining the original mission of these organizations. This book is the first step in reversing that trend."

—Rob Moll, editor-at-large, *Christianity Today*

"*Mission Drift* illustrates how organizations often lose their founding principles over time as they respond to the pressures of our secular culture and funding sensitivities. More important, *Mission Drift* gives useful tools and applications on how we can stay Mission True for the long term and breed excellence in application and execution as well."

—David Weekley, founder and chairman, David Weekley Homes

"No organization is exempt from the danger of drifting away from its original mission. While competing forces entice toward subtle changes, foundational principles must be safeguarded in your organization. In *Mission Drift*, Peter and Chris provide solid guidance for remaining laser-focused on core values—from the board level to daily organizational culture. This book is a timely message for any organization working hard to remain Mission True."

—Wess Stafford, president emeritus, Compassion International

"Whether you are flirting with the siren call of success and relevance, standing at an ethical fork in the road, undergoing massive growth, or reeling from previous highs, *Mission Drift* will help you and your key decision makers stay 'Mission True.'"

—Jeremy Courtney, author, *Preemptive Love: Pursuing Peace One Heart at a Time* and executive director, Preemptive Love Coalition

"Peter Greer and Chris Horst offer you a gift of supreme importance. Replete with examples. Practical in its message. Clarion in its call: Be Mission True or face the inevitable—Mission Drift."

—Robert Gelinas, lead pastor, Colorado Community Church and author, *The Mercy Prayer: The One Prayer Jesus Always Answers*

"I can't think of better leaders than Peter Greer and Chris Horst to teach us all a lesson on focus, intention, and staying power."

—Gabe Lyons, author, *The Next Christians* and founder, Q Ideas

"We have all seen Christian ministries go off track, either toward heresy or incompetence or irrelevance. This book shows us the other side with models of Christian ministries that have held fast to the Gospel and to their calling. Every Christian leader should reflect on the message of the book as we commit to keeping our mission in line with the mission of Christ."

—Russell Moore, president, Ethics and Religious
Liberty Commission

"Mission Drift is an enemy faced by every ministry. Incremental, insipid, and (nearly) invisible, it stealthily creeps up to envelop its prey. This book provides both a clarion warning and a clear pathway to stay true to the original call."

—Alec Hill, president, InterVarsity Christian Fellowship USA

"The Mission Drift message is timely and relevant for all who are seeking to make a difference in the world. Far too many once-successful efforts are carried off course by undercurrents of money, time, power, or ego, and one day find they've drifted miles from their point of origin. Peter Greer leads HOPE International with an unparalleled mission focus. This focus—and his passion for Christ-centered poverty alleviation—are why HOPE International is a key global mission partner for LifeChurch.tv."

—Cathi M. Linch, chief financial officer
and treasurer, LifeChurch.tv

"There are books that produce a much needed wake-up call, and there are books that inspire and propel. Incredibly, Peter Greer and Chris Horst have done both in *Mission Drift*. Guarding the missional heart of a ministry is both a calling and a privilege. *Mission Drift* challenges me to keep my finger on the pulse connected to the heartbeat of God for the stewardship of the Good News. Prepare to be challenged, encouraged, and commissioned."

—Dan Wolgemuth, president and CEO, Youth For Christ/USA

"With conviction and insight, Peter and Chris share with us their journey of discovery as they address the timely and pivotal question of Mission Drift. Their quest to get it right, not only for their personal integrity but for the longevity of the work in which they are engaged, informs our lives and our work as we endeavor to stay the course, finish well, and leave a legacy which continues to reflect kingdom values."

—Candy Sparks, executive director, The Crowell Trust

Books by Peter Greer

Mission Drift
(coauthored by Chris Horst with Anna Haggard)

The Spiritual Danger of Doing Good
(with Anna Haggard)

The Giver and the Gift

Mommy's Heart Went Pop!
(coauthored by Christina Kyllonen)

The Poor Will Be Glad
(coauthored by Phil Smith)

Dedicated to the men and women who faithfully
lead Mission True organizations

And to Laurel, Keith, Liliana & Myles and Alli & Desmond
for the abundant doses of grace, enthusiasm,
and love you share with us every day.

Contents

FOREWORD

Peter Greer and Chris Horst have identified one of the deepest challenges any leader faces: how to ensure that an organization stays true to its mission, especially when that mission becomes countercultural. And they squarely face a more specific challenge of our time: how to create lasting institutions that forthrightly place the proclamation of the Gospel of Jesus Christ at the heart of their mission.

I appreciate the way Peter and Chris are careful to affirm the good things that institutions do even without a faith commitment. The "Y" is a great place to play basketball, and basketball is a great part of being human. But Peter and Chris want us to ponder the path to the "Y" from the "YMCA." The Y has gradually elided not just three-quarters of its name, but much of its original Christian mission, and most traces of its founding history, from its institutional identity. What happened to the comprehensive vision of human flourishing that once might have placed the real good of basketball in a context of greater goods and God's ultimate good? Drift happened.

To be sure, one person (or generation)'s "drift" is another's "growth." But Peter and Chris remind us that too often, institutional drift is fundamentally unintended, the result not of sober and faithful choices in response to wider changes but simply unchosen, unreflective assimilation. Peter and Chris are not asking us to create organizations that never grow or change—they are asking us to create organizations that do not drift passively downstream when the cultural currents become swift.

They are marvelously honest about the sources of drift. Money plays a key role (as they remind us, you cannot understand the secularization of American colleges and universities without understanding the role of the Carnegie pension bequest). There is also the simple failure to pay attention at crucial moments, such as the selection of board members or the words we use to describe ourselves and our cause to diverse audiences. Most of all there is the scandal of the Gospel, which constantly calls all human beings and human institutions to repentance and transformation rather than accommodation and self-preservation.

This book addresses two dimensions of Mission Drift. The first kind is the drift that can happen on our watch, even under our very noses, when we take our mission for granted. The second is the drift that may or will happen after our watch, and direct influence, has ended.

The first kind is above all a call to personal humility and accountability. I found their reminder of why leaders fail—precisely at the moments when they seem to be succeeding—bracing and challenging. The greatest temptations, it seems, come at moments of great success or promise of success, the moments when it is easiest to forget our desperate need for God, without whom we can do nothing truly good or enduring.

The second kind of drift, meanwhile, is a call to *institutional* humility and accountability. I've had the opportunity to personally witness what happens at 11 a.m. in the offices of International Justice Mission, when meetings, email, and phone calls screech to a halt and the entire staff gathers for prayer. Peter and Chris describe the board members of the Crowell Trust taking time every single year to pray and read its founding funder's vision out loud. These are vivid examples of institutionalized humility (as strange as that phrase sounds)—practices that keep ambitious and energetic people grounded in something beyond themselves, something that came before and will endure after their momentary stewardship of the organization's mission.

The point of this book is not to denigrate or denounce the institutions that have changed, even from Christian roots, to become something quite different. Indeed, we need institutions that cross boundaries and barriers in our pluralistic, secular world, making room for faith without requiring it. I love Peter and Chris's appreciation for the genuine flourishing, and room for faith, that is possible at secularized institutions like Harvard University. There are still plenty of young Christian men who are called to play basketball at the Y, alongside neighbors who may not share their faith. Avoiding Mission Drift does not require us to retreat into safe, sectarian subcultures.

But some of us are called to tend earthen vessels that hold an incomparable treasure: the scandalous offer of grace from the world's Creator, through the sending and self-giving of the Son, in the power of the Spirit. Staying Mission True requires first of all that each of us become, personally, more and more deeply converted by this unlikely and beautiful mission. And then we are called, no doubt with fear and trembling, to do our best to build structures that will help that mission be encountered and believed long after we are gone.

Thankfully, this is not just our mission—in fact, in the most important sense it is not our mission at all. It is the mission of the One who will remain true even if all prove false, who has never drifted from His love and creative purpose. "The one who calls you is faithful, and he will do it."

—Andy Crouch

1

The Unspoken Crisis

Mission Drift is a crisis facing all faith-based organizations

Without careful attention, faith-based organizations will inevitably drift from their founding mission.

It's that simple. It will happen.

Slowly, silently, and with little fanfare, organizations routinely drift from their original purpose, and most will never return to their original intent. It has happened repeatedly throughout history and it was happening to us.

On the top floor of a Houston high-rise, I (Peter) sat across from a senior executive of a global oil and gas corporation. He led the company's charitable giving.

For over two years, we had cultivated this relationship. Late into many evenings, HOPE International staff members wrote reports to meet their deadlines. We even sent a field director to visit their London office—offering an inside glimpse of our microenterprise programs in sub-Saharan Africa. Until now, their financial support had been valuable, but relatively small scale.

But that could change. The executive articulated that he'd caught our vision. He wanted to help us provide business training, create savings accounts, and give small-business loans to many more under-resourced entrepreneurs in some of the most challenging countries in the world.

Rising from his seat, he said, "There is just one remaining issue." He paused. I held my breath.

"We are a publicly traded company and we cannot fund organizations that are so overtly faith based."

If our organization would tone down our Christian mission, his foundation would champion our cause. And we weren't talking pennies. They were ready to write a very large check. With their support, we could help many poor entrepreneurs throughout Africa and Asia pursue their dreams. Thousands—perhaps hundreds of thousands—more individuals could break the cycle of poverty.

I did not give an immediate response. Instead I thanked him for the offer and headed to the airport.

I didn't know what to do.

Everything in me wanted to make this work. We were friends. The company possessed extraordinary giving potential. I respected its leaders. And we were cash strapped.

Several of our board members initially encouraged us to explore a creative way to develop this partnership. For the good of our mission, couldn't we just "tone down" our Christian identity?

This began a critical conversation within our organization about Mission Drift. How does it happen? And more important, what can we do to prevent it? These questions prompted us to look around.

And what we found concerned us. Mission Drift wasn't just threatening us.

Pastor Training School

Consider this mission statement of a well-known university: "To be plainly instructed and consider well that the main end of your life and studies is to know God and Jesus Christ."

Founded in 1636, this university employed exclusively Christian professors, emphasized character formation in its students above all else, and rooted all its policies and practices in a Christian worldview. This school served as a bastion of academic excellence and Christian distinction.[1]

This mission statement, however, is not from Dallas Theological Seminary. Neither is it from Wheaton College. It's from *Harvard University*—this statement described their founding mission. Harvard began as a school to equip ministers to share the Good News.

Today, Harvard is an incredible institution with an unmatched reputation, but it no longer resembles its founding. A few years ago, I (Peter) attended Harvard for graduate school. I loved it. Dynamic and engaging, the professors and students alike pushed each other and eagerly sought to find solutions to the world's most challenging issues. I couldn't get enough. Some of my best memories were in Cambridge with faculty and friends.

My wife, Laurel, and I lived on Massachusetts Avenue and each morning, I hopped on my secondhand Schwinn bike, my books and laptop strapped to my back. When I neared the school, I watched the synchronized rowing of the Harvard crew slice through the water on the Charles River.

Watching them, you got the sense that a lot at Harvard hasn't changed since its founding.

Harvard is distinctly New England—and colonial New England at that. On my way to Swahili class at Sever Hall, I walked by John Harvard's statue. With his colonial garb, the university's first donor fit right in. From its architecture to its tradition, much of Harvard's legacy is still intact.

But Harvard's spiritual heritage is less visible. Aside from words on my diploma that read, *Christo et Ecclesiae* around *Veritas*, meaning "Truth for Christ and the Church," little evidence suggests it was a distinctly Christian school.

Mission Drift Defined

Only 80 years after its founding, Harvard's identity was shifting. A group of New England pastors sensed Harvard had drifted too far for their liking.[2] Concerned by the secularization at Harvard, they founded a new stronghold of Christian higher education in 1701.[3]

Clergyman Cotton Mather approached a wealthy philanthropist who shared their concerns. This man, Elihu Yale, financed their efforts in 1718, and they named the college after him, the institution today known as Yale University.[4]

Yale's motto was not just *Veritas* (truth) like Harvard, but *Lux et Veritas* (light and truth). These pastors hoped to avoid the drift they saw at Harvard.

But today, neither Harvard nor Yale resembles the universities their founders envisioned. At the 350th anniversary celebration of Harvard, Steven Muller, former president of Johns Hopkins University, didn't mince words: "The bad news is the university has become godless."[5]

Larry Summers, the president of Harvard while I was there, confirmed Muller's assessment, acknowledging, "Things divine have been central neither to my professional nor to my personal life."[6]

Our contention is not with the institutions Harvard and Yale are today. It's with the institutions they are not. Their founders were unmistakably clear in their goals: academic excellence and Christian formation. Today, they do something very different from their founding purpose. What happened to Harvard and Yale is the reality of Mission Drift.

Mission Drift unfolds slowly. Like a current, it carries organizations away from their core purpose and identity.

The changes at Harvard and Yale are dramatic, but they are not isolated incidents. The more we learned about Harvard and Yale, the more concerned we were about our own organization.

The Natural Course

Our decision point came when we'd been offered a very large check. In the boardroom, the executive's challenge—*tone down your Christian distinctiveness or forfeit our funding*—awakened us to the possibility of drift.

This potential major donor forced us to reexamine ourselves, to gain perspective, to take stock of where we were headed. This conversation was a gift that shaped the course of our organization more than any financial donation ever could.

After deciding to turn down this funding because we could not in good conscience "tone down" our Christian identity, we decided to go deeper in exploring where we might find the currents of Mission Drift.

Researching this key topic became our obsession and led us to the conclusion that Mission Drift isn't just a HOPE International problem. It's pervasive and affects faith-based organizations of all varieties—nonprofits, churches, denominations, businesses, foundations, and schools.

"It's the exception that an organization stays true to its mission," said Chris Crane, president and CEO of Edify. "The natural course— the unfortunate natural evolution of many originally Christ-centered missions—is to drift," he said.[7]

Franciscan Food Banks

The backdrop for our research is our industry. We work for HOPE International, a Christ-centered microenterprise development organization. Founded by a local church in response to needs in the former Soviet Union, our mission has always been to address material and spiritual needs in places of intense poverty.

By offering training, savings services, and small business loans through over 1,200 "missionary bankers," we actively share the Good News of Jesus Christ and equip families to work their way out of poverty. Today, across the HOPE global network, we serve over 600,000 clients in seventeen countries.

It seems inconceivable we would ever lose sight of our mission. But it is sobering to look at an ancient movement resembling our own and see how easy it is for Mission Drift to occur.

In the Middle Ages, the church sponsored a charity similar to modern-day urban food banks. Created as an alternative to loan sharks, *montes pietatius* helped poor people manage meager incomes.

These charities provided low-interest loans to poor families, ensuring there was enough food on the table. Started by the Franciscans, who opened more than one hundred fifty *montes pietatius*,[8] they became widespread throughout Europe. In 1514, even Pope Julius II gave an edict endorsing them.[9] The institutions were the lifeblood of poor European peasants.

Today, we know them as pawn shops.[10]

Pawn shops evolved from a tool designed to care for the needy to an instrument often preying on families in distress. Something intended for good drifted from its mission.

A few blocks from my (Chris's) house, a rundown pawn shop advertises its services to the low-income families who live in the neighborhood. I often drive by and see women and men at the point of desperation walking through the doors.

In the 1300s, people in poverty met caring friars when they entered the doors of pawn shops. The shops existed to help the poor get back on their feet, and these friars had their best interests in mind. Today, often the opposite is true.

Over time, pawn shop owners lost sight of their identity. Created for good, pawn shops have drifted away from their purpose.

In physics, a theory for drift exists. The second law of thermodynamics states that in the natural order of the universe, things degenerate, rather than come together. For example, when a frying pan is taken off the stove, heat diffuses in the air, leaving the pan cooler.

Unless heat is added—someone puts the frying pan back on the stove—it will cool and settle back to room temperature.[11] What we see in science (and the kitchen) we found to be the norm within organizations.[12]

Here's the reality: Mission Drift is the natural course for organizations, and it takes focused attention to safeguard against it. Once an organization ignores its source of heat, drift is only a matter of time.

Are We Adrift?

In a survey of hundreds of Christian leaders at the Q conference in Los Angeles in 2013, 95 percent said Mission Drift was a *challenging* issue to faith-based nonprofit organizations.[13]

As we began talking with Christian leaders, many recognized the pervasiveness of Mission Drift. Many lamented the drift they saw in their own organizations. Or they noted the ongoing challenges they faced in keeping their organizations on mission. But are we willing to ask the hard questions in order to address it?

It would be easy to write off Harvard and Yale's drift from their founding identity and purpose if they were exceptions. But Mission Drift is not relegated to the halls of Ivy League universities.

Mission Drift is a very real possibility for every organization. The zeal and beliefs of the founders are insufficient safeguards. There is no immunity, no matter how concrete your mission statement is. Or how passionate your leaders are. Or how much you believe it could never happen to you.

The more layers we peeled back, the more we began to see we were vulnerable. We discovered we'd already made compromises on our very DNA.

Though we had financial metrics, we didn't measure holistic transformation.

We had no way of formally assessing whether board members joining the organization bought into the full mission.

We didn't have structures to ensure our global staff members were in a vibrant relationship with Christ.

Our programs didn't systematically disciple or encourage spiritual growth in our staff members.

We had mission and vision statements but had not fully incorporated our beliefs into our culture and operations.

The Houston oil and gas corporation opened a window into the gravitational tug of Mission Drift. The deeper we looked, the more we learned faith-based organizations face the pull of secularization every day. In all facets of their missions.

In our self-exploration, we discovered we were making small decisions that, compounded over time, would lead to Mission Drift. If unchecked, we'd inevitably follow the pattern of organizations like Harvard and Yale.

Most organizations have not willingly, consciously, changed direction. Most have not volitionally chosen to soften their Christian distinctiveness. Neither Harvard nor Yale held a "mission change day" where they mapped out their new identity. Instead, they drifted quietly, gradually, and slowly. And one day, they hardly resembled the institutions their founders intended.

As we began looking at Harvard, Yale, and ourselves, we began to feel as if drift was inevitable. Is it even possible to stay distinctively Christian as you grow and professionalize? We began looking to our peers, hoping to find a path forward.

We found reasons to be optimistic that drift is not inevitable.

2

The Tale of Two
Presbyterian Ministers

Mission Drift is pervasive,
but it is not inevitable

An International Orphan Crisis

"Do you feel that Americans are doing all they can to help?"

Dr. J. Calvitt Clarke, a Presbyterian minister, asked the question of a friend who had been a missionary in China. Clarke knew the right answer. He had traveled enough to understand the plight of orphan children around the world.

His friend replied, "Why don't *you* do something about it?"

Clarke pondered the question, knowing his response would likely change his life forever. After a long pause, he responded confidently. "Alright. I will."[1]

Wars wreaked havoc throughout the world in the early 1900s. God-fearing men and women couldn't help but be moved by compassion to care for the vulnerable, the orphan, and the widow. They sought to address the suffering, disease, and poverty they saw. World Vision,

Compassion International, World Relief, and many other global ministries launched during the middle of the twentieth century.

The Birth of Child Sponsorship

One of these organizations was China's Children's Fund. After his conversation with his former missionary friend, Calvitt Clarke founded the
organization in 1938. Clarke was a man of deep convictions about the
poor. He had traveled on a number of mission trips around the world and
had been affected most by the suffering of innocent children.[2] The first
outreach from his new organization was to Chinese children in response
to the orphan crisis following the Sino-Japanese War. The ministry
expanded and soon changed its name to Christian Children's Fund.[3]

Clarke cared deeply about ministering the Gospel in word and deed
to orphaned children in China. To fund the efforts, Clarke invented
child sponsorship, an innovative approach built around connecting
donors directly to individual children.[4]

Clarke's organization escalated to charity celebrity status. Throughout the 1980s and early 1990s, Christian Children's Fund was all
over television. They ran lengthy documentary infomercials hosted
by Hollywood pseudo-star Sally Struthers.

During the shows, Struthers covered provocative and tragic stories
of global poverty, famine, and war. By 1994, the organization served
nearly 2 million children through child sponsorships with a budget of
over 100 million dollars.[5] In 2011 *Forbes* named Christian Children's
Fund one of the 100 largest charities in the country.[6]

An Identity Crisis

But by the 1990s, Christian Children's Fund's very identity was called
into question. In an interview with *Christianity Today*, Thomas Nay-
lor, a former board member, said, "This organization has nothing to
do with Christianity."[7]

A decade later, a charity watchdog issued a "donor alert," warning Christian Children's Fund may be "misleading many Christian
donors" because of its marketing as a Christian organization.[8]

Its president, Anne Goddard, acknowledged the change in the identity of the organization: "An organization changes slowly, and then all of a sudden you realize the changes have happened so much that you need to step back and [see if you are] putting out the name that really reflects who you are."[9]

In 2009, it changed its name to ChildFund International.[10]

The Second Presbyterian Minister

Just over a decade after Clarke founded China Children's Fund, a fellow Presbyterian minister, Everett Swanson,[11] visited orphans in war-torn Korea. A missionary friend asked him a dangerous question: "You have seen the tremendous needs and unparalleled opportunities of this land: What do you intend to do about it?"[12]

Swanson was in Korea often. Following the Korean War in the early 1950s, he preached the Gospel throughout the country, wherever he was invited: training camps, military academies, and detention centers.

At the time, the Koreans were a people uprooted—broken by the horrors of war. Through these challenges, tens of thousands professed faith in Christ. Swanson began to mourn for more than the hearts of the Korean people. He grieved that war had ravaged the country, propelling millions into abject poverty. Specifically, he lamented the plight of Korean children. Approximately 100,000 were orphaned from the war.[13]

"On the cold nights, they are found on the streets, alleys, doorways, and so forth, but these boys are precious in the eyes of the Lord. And Christ died to save them," said Swanson.

Swanson walked the streets of Seoul daily, praying for these hurting children. One morning, with the cold air stinging his face, Swanson saw policemen scoop up piles of rags from a street corner. As he walked closer, he realized these were not rags, but orphans who had died in the freezing conditions overnight.[14]

The experience haunted him. Swanson couldn't rid his mind of the images.

What do you intend to do about it?

The question burned in his heart. He began asking this question of others. In each church where he spoke, he challenged the congregants to respond to the needs of the people of Korea, not knowing he was creating an organization as he did so. But this simple question planted the seeds of Compassion International. In 1952, Swanson and his passionate sponsors provided food, education, clothing, and spiritual nourishment to a group of thirty-five orphaned and vulnerable children in Korea.

Today, Compassion International serves over 1.3 million children across twenty-six countries. Compassion helps them through local churches, improving their health, education, and life skills, and introducing these children to Jesus Christ.[15]

Reverend Everett Swanson knew his purpose. He founded Compassion to provide for the social, material, and spiritual needs of at-risk youth around the world. Today, over sixty years later, Compassion precisely embodies Swanson's convictions. And their commitment to the Gospel has not waned. It has only grown more resolute as Compassion has aged.

Despite facing an onslaught of pressures to drift from its founding identity, Compassion hasn't backed down from its core purpose of meeting not only the material, but also the spiritual needs of children. Wess Stafford, president of Compassion International from 1993–2013, reflected:

> When I was the director of development at Compassion back in the 1980s, I brought in outside experts to study our marketing and donor base. I asked, "What do we need to do to grow?" I'll never forget their answer: "Well, you've got the best name in the business, 'Compassion International.' Who doesn't want to be a part of something called Compassion? But you've got this Jesus stuff mixed in there. Not everyone compassionate cares about this Jesus that you keep putting out with every piece of material. Our advice is really raise up the name Compassion and sort of soft sell the Jesus stuff. Then watch what can happen."
>
> We thought for ten seconds, and said, "No, not now, not ever."[16]

The reason Swanson founded Compassion is the reason Compassion exists today. Compassion has remained *Mission True*. Their story gave us great hope. They figured out how to protect their mission. They understood their Christian identity and built safeguards around it.

On the surface, ChildFund and Compassion International look like twins. They were founded just fourteen years apart. Both were started by Presbyterian ministers, each with a passion for helping the poor. Both founders had missionary friends who encouraged them to start their organizations. Both were created to help children orphaned after wars in Asia, one in China and the other in Korea. Both use child sponsorship to fuel their missions.

While we read the stories of their foundings, we couldn't believe the parallels. These two organizations could not have started out more similarly. And today, both are among the 100 largest nonprofits in the country. But they now look radically different. One—ChildFund—stripped "Christian" from its very name. The other—Compassion—beats to the same heartbeat as its founder. How did Compassion manage to protect its identity, even as it grew to become one of the largest charities in the world?

Mission True Defined

The more we learned about Compassion, the more we were encouraged. We began looking for more organizations like them. Finding and celebrating Mission True organizations became our passion. So what is a Mission True organization?

> In its simplest form, Mission True organizations know why they exist and protect their core at all costs. They remain faithful to what they believe God has entrusted them to do. They define what is immutable: their values and purposes, their DNA, their heart and soul.

This doesn't mean Mission True organizations don't change. And it doesn't mean they aren't striving for excellence. In fact, their understanding of their core identity will demand they change. And their understanding of Scripture will demand they strive for the very highest levels of excellence. But growth and professionalism are subordinate values. To remain Mission True is to adapt and grow, so long as that adaptation and growth does not alter the core identity.

To find these organizations, we began asking experts—educators, philanthropists, ministry leaders, and pastors—"Which organizations have remained Mission True?" Dozens of recommendations came back from many different sectors. And we compiled a list of the most commonly recommended organizations. We interviewed them about their secrets to remaining Mission True. (Details of our research can be found at the back of the book.)

We invested hundreds of hours listening to and learning from these organizations. They were diverse. Some were prominent institutions like Compassion, an organization with over a half-billion-dollar[17] annual budget. Some were lesser known, but just as compelling, like Taylor University, a small college located in the cornfields of Indiana. Taylor has faithfully stayed the course for over one hundred fifty years.

Some deployed nearly identical practices as they did at their founding, including The Crowell Trust, a charitable foundation that acts today nearly exactly as it acted in its earliest days in the 1930s. Others have changed dramatically. Young Life, a national youth ministry, initially reached children through barbershop quartets. Their methods have changed significantly over the years, but they have not lost their heart and founding commitment to share Christ with young people.

Some were overtly evangelistic, like InterVarsity, Cru, and Youth For Christ, an organization that first put Billy Graham on a stage and today still exists to introduce young people to Jesus Christ. Others were just as faithful, but fulfilled a different mandate. National Christian Foundation—now the third largest donor-advised fund in the world—is rooted and sustained by their conviction about the Gospel, but they operate much differently than the aforementioned organizations. We wish we could have featured all our favorite faith-based organizations in this book, but we limited ourselves to prevent it from becoming too lengthy.

Flippant Carefrontations

While in an idyllic camp setting, I (Peter) participated in an event with other followers of Jesus eager to positively impact culture. Our goals were to encourage one another and deepen relationships. On the last evening we shared highlights of our time together. The gathering was replete with memorable conversations.

Near the end of the night, one member stood up and began pointing out the flaws of our group. He critiqued the leaders, bemoaned the structure, and challenged our motivations.

Backs stiffened. Jaws clenched.

He hadn't earned the right to criticize. He hadn't been invited to critique. His "carefrontation" came from a position of self-righteousness. And so no one listened. His words created a stir but did not encourage any positive change.

It isn't our intent to offer unsolicited critique. This book is written to equip Christians "in the trenches" who believe Mission Drift is (or could be) a concern. If you are a donor, board member, or staff member at an organization you fear is adrift, we hope this book will equip you to help your favorite ministry stay true to its mission.

Even uglier than finger-pointing is when someone tries to prove they are "more Christian" than someone else. We do not intend to hold up our organization as an ideal. We all have enough planks in our own eyes to pull out before examining the specks of dust in our friends' eyes.[18]

A third concern in writing *Mission Drift* is this: Some may interpret this book as an exposé of organizations that have drifted. That's not our intent either. This book is not a witch-hunt. You won't find a "Top 10 Drifting Organizations" list. You won't find any scathing reveals of organizations in the midst of identity crises. Though we profile organizations throughout, we very intentionally chose organizations that have publicly and widely communicated their own drift. Their leaders have openly acknowledged their shifting identity.

The boards and presidents at Harvard, Yale, and ChildFund are neither embarrassed nor private about their drift: They affirm and celebrate it. They believe in their new identity.

From our interviews, we know many organizations are currently wrestling with Mission Drift, but we purposefully avoided mentioning them. We hope this will be a resource for anyone eager to protect and reinforce their mission. The stories of drift we share are meant to edify, and in no way humiliate or disparage.

Finally, we're concerned this book could undermine organizations we celebrate as Mission True. We have failed in writing *Mission Drift* if we create the impression that these organizations are immune to drift. We have put these organizations and their leaders in greater jeopardy if this book makes them think they have arrived. Remaining Mission True is a constant pursuit. As in the second law of thermodynamics, cooling is inevitable unless leaders regularly infuse heat and energy into fueling and safeguarding their missions.

If this book reads like the overzealous and self-righteous friend eager to critique others or makes Mission True organizations take pride in their accomplishments, we will have failed those who have drifted and failed those who have remained true. If *Mission Drift* becomes a bully stick for boards and leaders—in either direction—we have dreadfully missed the mark.

Our aims are fairly simple. We want to name and illustrate the causes of Mission Drift. We want to help you clarify the missions of the organizations you most love. And we want to equip you with the safeguards to reinforce and protect them.

Choose This Day

Mission True organizations decide that their identity matters and then become fanatically focused on remaining faithful to this core.

The key to Mission True organizations isn't a charismatic leader. If it was, they'd have Mission Drift within the second generation if the inevitable leadership transition wasn't flawless. Compassion and the other organizations we profile in this book do not possess a mysterious set of practices and principles only applicable to them. Rather, their practices are transferrable to any organization, denomination, or ministry. These are what we identified as Mission True qualities.

We hope that these observations and supporting stories will compel you to consider the implications of ignoring the crisis lurking in all our organizations and, even deeper, in our hearts. Our research led us to an uncomfortable conclusion: The pressures of Mission Drift are guaranteed. It is the default, the auto-fill. It *will happen* unless we are focused and actively preventing it.

In marriage, if we stop working on our relationship and just rely on the spark we had during our early days, we know how the story will end. In a similar way, organizations relying on the zeal of their founders will experience Mission Drift if they aren't actively and regularly working to protect and enhance the mission.

Will we choose to do the hard work of protecting our mission?

After leading the Israelites into the Promised Land, Joshua knew his nation stood at a decision point. After laying out their history, he made it clear that they had a choice to make:

> But if serving the Lord seems undesirable to you, then choose for yourselves this day whom you will serve, whether the gods your ancestors served beyond the Euphrates, or the gods of the Amorites, in whose land you are living. But as for me and my household, we will serve the Lord.[19]

Mission Drift and You

In writing this book, we changed our hypothesis. Initially, we saw Mission Drift as an organizational issue. But as organizations are made up of individuals foiled by pride and sin and allured by success, we concluded that this unspoken crisis isn't an organizational problem. It's a human one. We found Mission Drift wouldn't be a problem if humans weren't involved. But alas all organizations—every last one of them—have humans at the helm.

God has called us to lives of faithfulness. And this is the lifeblood of Mission True organizations.

At the end of his life, Paul said to his son in the faith, Timothy, "I have fought the good fight, I have finished the race, I have kept the faith."[20]

What a striking statement. While Paul knew he was far from perfect—even calling himself the "worst" of sinners[21]—he had an undivided heart, one grounded in the recognition of Christ's unlimited love. Through Christ, Paul did everything in his power to remain obedient to his mission.

Our hope for us, for you, your organizations, your church, your ministry—these missions you love and support—is to do the same.

The Gospel of Jesus Christ is the very thing our world so desperately needs. And the infusion of the Gospel in our organizations is what we most need to protect. Surprisingly, it took a journalist, a Hollywood star, a rabbi, and an atheist to remind us why.

3

FUNCTIONAL ATHEISM

Mission True organizations believe the Gospel is their most precious asset

"Is it really worth trying to integrate your personal faith into your organization?" a friend recently asked.

He appropriately recognized how difficult it is to carry out quality poverty alleviation work in challenging places. Addressing matters of the heart only increases the challenge. It makes it harder to recruit staff. It closes certain funding opportunities. It adds costs.

If it's going to be more difficult, we need to fully believe in its importance because we will be challenged. If we aren't entirely convinced that our Christian faith is essential to our work, then we won't be willing to make the tough decisions to fight for it.

Sometimes we can take for granted the things we should most value. This is definitely true when it comes to protecting our Christian distinctiveness in our organizations. Sometimes it's the unlikeliest voices that have the most to teach us.

The Ugly Secret of Poverty

In 2010, *New York Times* columnist Nicholas Kristof visited the Republic of Congo. Traveling around the country, he captured inspiring signs of hope. However, he also unearthed a reality few are willing to verbalize:

> There's an ugly secret of global poverty, one rarely acknowledged by aid groups or U.N. reports. It's a blunt truth that is politically incorrect, heartbreaking, frustrating and ubiquitous: It's that if the poorest families spent as much money educating their children as they do on wine, cigarettes and prostitutes, their children's prospects would be transformed.[1]

We work in Congo. We know some of the complexities of poverty. And we know poverty cannot be solved merely by shipments of food, pioneering malaria treatments, or the construction of new homes. To achieve lasting change, people in poverty need work. They need jobs. We recognize many suffer primarily because of lack of opportunities. We committed our careers to providing men and women the financial tools and training they need to lift themselves out of poverty.

But as Kristof laments, the ugly secret of poverty remains. Jobs and increased incomes are not solutions in themselves. Prosperity can actually contribute to *more* brokenness.

More Prostitutes and Liquor

The first time I (Peter) encountered the ugly secret was while managing a microfinance program in Rwanda. Jean-Paul[2] was one of the first people I helped to kick-start a small business.

Early in our relationship, I visited Jean-Paul. His home stood in a dilapidated state of disrepair. His children didn't attend school. His household was a portrait of poverty. And my job was to invest in people like him.

I helped Jean-Paul start a small market stand business selling garments and soap and gave him the basic business training and capital he needed to get the business up and running. And Jean-Paul took off. His income surged and his business expanded.

After he achieved business success, I visited him again. As I walked the dusty road to his home, I expected to see a renovated house. I anticipated meeting joyful kids, textbooks in hand. I quietly hoped to snap my picture with his gleeful children.

But there was no change. His kids weren't in school. His home showed no improvements. He was making money, but his home and family still communicated an image of poverty.

Later, I learned that Jean-Paul used his increased profits on prostitutes and alcohol. His business success and increased income did not improve his life and did not make life better for his family. Having dedicated the last several years of my life to economic development, I experienced incredible disappointment.

I moved to Africa to serve the Lord and try to make a lasting impact. But I was simply helping Jean-Paul consume more liquor and abuse more women trapped in prostitution. Talk about a sobering realization. It forced me to question everything, and it reinforced Kristof's ugly secret. I realized that he was correct: "If we're going to make more progress . . . we need to look unflinchingly at uncomfortable truths."[3] Jean-Paul's life presented an uncomfortable truth indeed.

Apart from Christ, we might simply introduce the problems of prosperity while we solve the problems of poverty. Jean-Paul's increased wealth made his conditions even worse.

An Atheist Enabled Me to Believe

It was an atheist who convinced me (Chris) that our world needs more than just good humanitarianism.

Matthew Parris, a British journalist, wrote in the *London Times*, "As an atheist, I truly believe Africa needs God." In a day and age in which many in our society believe Christianity to be irrelevant (at best) or dangerous (at worst), Parris's conviction shocked me. In his article he repeatedly asserted his unbelief in God, *but* he admitted that his own beliefs are insufficient to solve the issues of corruption and poverty in our world.

Shortly after a trip to Africa, he wrote:

> Now a confirmed atheist, I've become convinced of the enormous
> contribution that Christian evangelism makes in Africa: sharply distinct
> from the work of secular NGOs, government projects and international
> aid efforts. These alone will not do. Education and training alone
> will not do. In Africa Christianity changes people's hearts. It brings
> a spiritual transformation. The rebirth is real. The change is good.[4]

Parris is clear: the message of Jesus is the solution. Christianity
frees people. African Christians stand tall because they know they are
made in God's image. They understand their personal responsibility
to make a difference in their communities. They submit to a higher
moral code.

Beyond Humanitarianism

Scholars Michael Barnett and Janice Gross Stein make the bold statement that "it is only a slight exaggeration to say 'no religion, no
humanitarianism.'"[5] They take a different tack but reinforce what
both Kristof and Parris acknowledged.

Barnett and Stein's edited compilation *Sacred Aid* identifies why
faith-based organizations are distinct. What advantage do contempo-
rary faith-based organizations possess over their secular counterparts?

Stamina. "Those driven by religious faith also might be more willing to endure hardship and personal sacrifice for a longer period of
time."[6]

With a long-term commitment in view, faith-based organizations
are often more deeply rooted in the lands where they work. It is no
surprise, then, that Nicholas Kristof, the *New York Times* reporter
who noticed poverty's ugly secret, could report that "the further he
travels from the capital city, the greater is the likelihood the aid worker
he meets will be from a religious organization."[7]

Why is this so? What is the source of the resilience that drives
religious organizations into these difficult places? And why do they
succeed where secular organizations fail? The answer lies in differing
objects of faith. Bertrand Taithe is instructive here: "Faith in mankind

is harder to sustain than faith in God. In highly competitive humanitarian markets, this is their main advantage."[8]

When tragedy strikes, and victims are forced to grapple with the truth of their own mortality, "the language of the sacred—forbearance, mystery, suffering, hope, finitude, surrender, divine purpose, and redemption—and the mechanisms of religion become more relevant."[9]

Where secular organizations place their faith in the human person, religious organizations recognize that human persons—divorced from God—can never truly deal with the problems most fundamental to human society. Poverty may be alleviated, but prosperity brings its fair share of problems along with it.

Following the 2011 London riots, Jonathan Sacks, Britain's chief rabbi, wrote in the *Wall Street Journal* about the importance of religion in bringing about social order and flourishing societies:

> Much can and must be done by governments, but they cannot of themselves change lives. Governments cannot make marriages or turn feckless individuals into responsible citizens. That needs another kind of change agent. . . . It needs religion: not as doctrine but as a shaper of behavior, a tutor in morality, an ongoing seminar in self-restraint and pursuit of the common good.[10]

As the rabbi said, faith often provides a framework to address societal ills such as isolation, anarchy, and fear. We would go further: "Aid" divorced from the context of faith fails to deal with humanity's most basic problem. Secular relief is just that—relief; it does not and cannot address those issues that are most fundamental to the human condition.

Celebrity Endorsement

In an interview with *Rolling Stone* in 1999, Brad Pitt shared candidly about the shortcomings of the world's definition of success. He lamented the rise in secularism, saying, "We are heading for a dead end, a numbing of the soul, a complete atrophy of the spiritual being."

Chris Heath, reporter for *Rolling Stone,* followed up and asked Pitt, "So if we're heading toward this kind of existential dead end in society, what do you think should happen?" Pitt replied,

Hey, man, I don't have those answers yet. The emphasis now is on success and personal gain. [*Smiles*] I'm sitting in it, and I'm telling you,
that's not it. . . . I'm the guy who's got everything. I know. But I'm telling
you, once you get everything, then you're just left with yourself. I've
said it before and I'll say it again: It doesn't help you sleep any better,
and you don't wake up any better because of it. Now, no one's going
to want to hear that. I understand it. I'm sorry I'm the guy who's got
to say it. But I'm telling you.[11]

Pitt states a similar ugly truth as Kristof—the pursuit of wealth
and acclaim always comes up short.

An atheist, a Jewish rabbi, a columnist from *The New York Times*,
and an American celebrity—it almost sounds like the start to a bad
joke—all recognize that without heart change, money, health care,
housing, and education do not meet our world's deepest needs.

What Is the Core Distinction?

Christians understand the importance of Good Samaritanism. In
Jesus' parable, the character of the Good Samaritan exhibits a lifestyle
of service that isn't intuitive: Inconvenient and often dangerous, this
extravagant charity does not profit him.

In a book about Mission Drift, then, we begin with a call to the
Christian church—an appeal to remember that we are not just world-
class humanitarians, but Christians. We must do good, but we must not
forget we have *Good News* to share. Do we still believe this news matters? Do we believe it is the best news the world could ever be told? We
believe a commitment to this news is precisely what keeps us on mission.

The early followers of Jesus cared for those abandoned to die from
an epidemic plague that began in 165 A.D. and claimed the lives of
up to a third of the population in the Roman Empire.[12] During the
Middle Ages, a charity revolution initiated by Christians led to the
founding of hundreds of hospitals across Europe.[13] These hospitals
not only cared for the sick and dying, but also welcomed the homeless.

Nineteenth-century missionaries built schools in Africa. Church
groups build wells in these same countries today. Christians have been
the lifeblood of charity work across the nation and throughout the

world. Christian hospitals, universities, schools, and community centers dot rural and urban landscapes.

Christians volunteer, teach, and serve at-risk youth and elderly
widows. According to Arthur C. Brooks, president of the American
Enterprise Institute, "Religious people are 25 percentage points more
likely than secularists to donate money (91 percent to 66 percent) and
23 points more likely to volunteer time (67 percent to 44 percent)."[14]

As followers of Jesus Christ, we carry a rich legacy of good deeds,
but do we believe we offer far more than our serving hands and willing
checkbooks? Do we really believe Christ is *the* difference?

In *Sacred Aid*, scholars Barnett and Stein revealed results similar
to what we found in our research: "Over the course of the twentieth
century, the secularization of humanitarianism only increased, and
by the 1970s the movement's religious inspiration, generally speaking,
was marginal to its agenda."[15]

Pointing to the Kingdom

Jesus was more than just a moral teacher. Weaving His teaching with
miracles, He demonstrated that He was the promised Messiah.

In John 6, we read the familiar story of Jesus feeding the 5,000
with only five barley loaves and two fish. Later He told the crowd,
"I am the bread of life; whoever comes to me shall not hunger, and
whoever believes in me shall never thirst."[16] This was a prophetic sign
announcing that the Messiah, the Rescuer, had come.

Throughout His life, Jesus did numerous other miracles to give
glimpses of His Kingdom. In the Kingdom of Heaven, there won't
be any sickness. So Jesus healed the sick. In the Kingdom of Heaven,
there won't be any hunger. So Jesus fed the 5,000. In the Kingdom
of Heaven, there won't be any death. So Jesus raised Lazarus and a
little girl from the dead.

Christ regularly pointed to His divinity by acts that give a taste
of what the Kingdom will be like. Yes, Jesus did good works—but
there was a bigger reason behind them. Through His life, death, and
resurrection, He announced He was the promised Messiah. Forgive-
ness and new life are available for all who trust in Him.

By believing Jesus is the Savior, we are released from the bond-
age of sin, are given an eternal hope, become heirs with Christ, are
declared without blemish,[17] and are given a foundation for selfless
service to those in need.

With such Good News, why aren't we passionately sharing this
message while we serve?

Muting Jesus

Few people are less qualified to speak at a Princeton University conference in Austria than I (Chris). Even prestigious universities make
mistakes, however, and I received an invitation. In the preconference
packet, lofty bios of policy makers, leaders of international organizations, and academics filled the pages. My bio followed a former U.S.
ambassador's.

I felt like a computer programmer at a bodybuilding convention. But
I was happy to put my bachelor's degree in sports management and
two and a half years of professional experience to work. The Wood-
row Wilson School of Public and International Affairs at Princeton
University (or TWWSOPAIAAPU for short) hosted the conference
on the topic "Faith and International Development."

We hailed from many faith persuasions. We enjoyed quintessential
Vienna sausages and even watched a full orchestra perform a concert
on the lawn of the breathtaking Schönbrunn Palace. Our week was
enjoyable, and during the sessions, we debated the issues amicably. But
there was one presenter who irked me. Said more clearly, he attacked me.

In his presentation, he said that Christian evangelism is dangerous,
paternalistic, and wildly inappropriate. He argued that the sanctuary is the only venue where Jesus-talk is permissible. And he had a
scathing rebuke for international organizations who claimed otherwise. Earlier in the day, I had described HOPE's approach and why
we believed the full integration of our faith was so critical. I made it
clear we believed in evangelism.

He critiqued the way some faith-based organizations address matters of the heart. While he flipped through his slides, I felt as if the
entire group of prestigious intellectuals was staring at me. I cowered

in the corner, embarrassed by the scolding the more senior and highly credentialed presenter was giving me.

In retrospect, I sure wish this guy could have talked with Brad Pitt. Pitt described secularism as a "dead end, a numbing of the soul." Pitt has it all. Yet he knows that even a Whole Foods diet, an Ivy League education, safe housing, and clean water do not salve life's pains.

Here is what was most disappointing about this interaction and many others I've had like it: It's often Christians who seem most likely to be the biggest critics of bold Christian distinctiveness in our organizations. The presenter was the only other Christian presenting at the conference. And he hailed from a peer faith-based organization.

Our Most Precious Asset

ChildFund changed their name in a dramatic display of Mission Drift. But their drift didn't happen overnight. The current of secularism progressively carried them off course. Today, ChildFund provides education, health care, and nutrition to at-risk children in the United States and abroad. But their work does not resemble what their founders intended. They no longer address all the needs children have. They fill children's bellies, but ignore their hearts.

ChildFund's story is not an anomaly. And these stories are not just past tense. They are all around us. Dr. Wess Stafford, president and CEO of Compassion International, said, "I can think of many Christian organizations that have lost their spiritual commitment. I can't think of one secular organization that found its way to a Christian commitment. Any leader who inherits a strong Christian commitment must shepherd the culture and steward that commitment."[18]

Christian leaders are often quiet about the crisis in our boardrooms, hiring practices, and fundraising strategies. The gravitational forces of secularization tug at us from all sides, beckoning us to abandon the "Jesus stuff" and to focus solely on adoption services, educating youth, and curing the sick. As if we can do these things in a values-neutral sort of way.

Operating in this fashion, we deploy what theologian James K. A. Smith describes as *functional secularism*.[19] We aren't secular in our own convictions as Christians, but often our organizations sure look like they are. Scholar Bryant Myers went further. He said many of our faith-based organizations aren't just functionally secularist—they're *functionally atheist.*[20] These are issues that the largest faith-based organizations in the world grapple with. Both publicly and privately, their leaders acknowledged that these issues are hotly discussed. Paradoxically, it is often voices *outside* the Church who seem to call us to remain Mission True and remember what makes us distinct.

"Ministries need to remember how important it is not to sell off the vision when times are tough," reflected Fred Smith, president of The Gathering, a community of Christian givers actively providing comfort, challenge, and cheering on to people all over the world, as well as one another. "It's like selling the family heirlooms. You have some money but the loss is enormous."[21]

Are we trading away our most precious asset? While Christian faith-based organizations feel pressure to abandon their faith, many non-Christians ask us to consider our roots. They recognize Christ as the very One who enables us to better address the needs of our world. They plead for us to look at the perils of drifting away from our source.

As Matthew Parris—the atheist journalist—concluded in the *London Times*, "Removing Christian evangelism from the African equation may leave the continent at the mercy of a malign fusion of Nike, the witch doctor, the mobile phone and the machete."[22]

Mission True Organizations

If we continue to apologize for our faith, conceal its importance, and drift from our core, we will lose the very uniqueness our world so desperately needs. Mission True organizations:

1. *Recognize that Christ is the difference.* Mission True organizations humbly acknowledge that education, experience, and the latest technology are not enough to transform hearts and lives. Without heart change, prosperity can lead to more brokenness.

2. *Affirm that faith sustains them.* As Barnett and Stein assert in *Sacred Aid*, faith gives organizations endurance, often making

them more effective than their secular counterparts. Faith empowers Mission True organizations to face obstacles in dark times.

3. *Understand that functional atheism is the path of least resistance.* Without a disciplined reliance on God in methodologies and daily practices, Mission True organizations can readily become Christian in name alone.

The Good Samaritan movement is in danger of forgetting that if we abandon Jesus, we lose everything.

But if we decide to safeguard the centrality of the Gospel in our organizations, we should be prepared. By committing ourselves to Jesus, it might seem we are going to lose everything.

4

DEATH BY MINNOWS

Mission True organizations make hard
decisions to protect and propel their mission

It was supposed to be a joyous day at Southern Baptist Theological
Seminary. But a dummy swinging from the tree outside the chapel
door signaled tension.

This was a divided campus.[1]

Delivering the convocation address was Dr. Albert Mohler's first
task as the newly elected president of the storied seminary. But his first
day was not a simple torch passing. At the time, Southern was known
as a drifting seminary. Mohler's appointment signaled a change. It
was a new day and a new direction for an institution at a crossroads.[2]

When the board introduced the 33-year-old Dr. Mohler to the
student body a few months earlier, many students stood and turned
their backs to the podium. Indifference to Dr. Mohler's appointment
did not exist. Volatility surged among students, alumni, and faculty
as they debated the board's decision.

With his effigy swinging outside the window, Dr. Mohler stood in
front of tenured faculty and students to lay out his intentions for the

institution—that they return to their original mission and honor the
Abstract of Principles, Southern's confession of faith:

> Let those who would understand Southern Seminary understand
> this: . . . That this Abstract is a sacred contract and confession for
> those who teach here—who willingly and willfully affix their signatures
> to its text and their conscience to its intention. They pledge to teach
> "in accordance with and not contrary to" its precepts.[3]

Southern had drifted far from its founding. When he attended the
seminary years earlier, Dr. Mohler "had professors that . . . openly
questioned any notion of a bodily resurrection. They looked dismis-
sively at the virgin birth, denied the Trinity. . . . Human sinfulness
had been redefined."[4]

For these and other reasons, Dr. Mohler drew the lines that day. He
insisted that all faculty members abide by the Abstract, which they
had signed, and over the course of the next year, most of the faculty
members were fired or resigned. Incalculable millions of donor dollars were lost. Student enrollment dipped to historic lows. Southern
Seminary stood on the precipice. "I said," Dr. Mohler reflected, "if
this is what you believe, then we want you to stay. If not, then you
have come here under false pretenses, and you must go."[5]

Today, Southern Seminary is "one of the world's largest theological
seminaries."[6] Regardless of whether you agree with the seminary's
theology, Dr. Mohler's effigy tells us something about the challenges
leaders are up against when they return their organizations to their
founding identities.

Dr. Mohler met significant challenges in his first year at Southern.
His opponents fought with ferocity. But he chose the immense pain of
his first year over the inevitable slow decline that would have resulted
from ignoring his institution's lingering inconsistencies. He knew well
the stories of Harvard, Yale, and dozens of other American colleges
and seminaries. And he would not allow this same drift to unfold at
Southern Seminary.

"Getting eaten by a whale or nibbled to death by minnows results
in the same thing," said Steve Haas, vice president at World Vision,
"although one demise is typically more difficult to diagnose."[7]

Dr. Mohler refused to let Southern Seminary die by minnows.

Floating Along

When school let out, in the Greer family it meant the camp season was about to begin. For at least ten consecutive summers, our family would head north from Massachusetts, cross into New Hampshire, and keep driving until we reached Camp Brookwoods and Deer Run on Lake Winnipesaukee.

On one of our camp excursions, we had to canoe across Eagle Lake in the Allagash Wilderness at the northern tip of Maine. A slight breeze made the August day feel delightfully cool. We casually paddled, but mostly were caught up in conversation and using our oars to splash the other canoes. We sang a little. We munched our gorp and other snacks. Quintessential camp life.

But we didn't go very far. The currents and winds silently counteracted our feeble efforts. As the day wore on, the wind really picked up. By the afternoon, there were surging whitecaps. Small talk ended. We put our heads down and rowed with all our might. But we weren't moving at all.

While the sun was out, we had spent the morning going at a relaxed and leisurely pace. Now we were working our very hardest and making little progress. We decided to put up camp and weather the storm overnight.

Crossing the lake, we eventually made it to the river. Here, we faced a completely different situation. Paddling was not a concern as the river narrowed and sucked us into the foamy whitewater. Navigating around rocks, our small canoes journeyed where the currents took us.

The Allagash canoe trip taught me to never underestimate the currents and the winds. You pay attention to them because they have their own agendas. You ignore them at your own peril. And at times, you have to fight with all your might not to let them take you to places you don't want to go.

Plotting Mission Drift

Our initial research into Mission True organizations surprised us. In the interviews we conducted, the first response we heard was almost always "Mission Drift is a daily battle."

As we heard the stories, we developed a simple framework. It's not perfect, but it helped us categorize the organizations. On a grid, we plotted two variables:

1. Clarity of Christian mission
2. Intentionality of safeguarding it

In other words: *Do you know who you are?* and *Are you protecting your identity?*

For organizations analyzed on this grid, we assume Christian distinctiveness is of concern and importance to the organization and its leaders. We believe the principles of this book—and this model—hold implications for organizations of all flavors. But we wrote this book specifically and directly for and to leaders of evangelical faith-based nonprofit organizations.

Though imperfect, the following questionnaire will help you assess the clarity of your mission, the safeguards in place, and how susceptible you are to Mission Drift.

Mission Drift Survey

Please rate yourself on a scale of 1 to 10.

1 = Strongly Disagree
5 = Neither Agree nor Disagree
10 = Strongly Agree

CLARITY

1. Mission Drift is a topic of conversation within your organization.
2. The verbal sharing of Christ is actively and intentionally being discussed/encouraged on a consistent basis (even if methods for doing so are less clear because of context limitations).
3. Your organization has a statement of belief, mission statement, and core documents that explicitly describe its full mission.
4. Staff members know and believe the core tenets of your full mission.
5. Supporters are in alignment with the core tenets of your full mission.

6. Your key donors are vocal and engaged in keeping you accountable to remaining on mission. (For example, they speak up and
   challenge leadership if something does not clearly articulate or
   embody your values.)

7. Board members and staff sign a statement of faith before joining
   the board/organization.

8. You have consistency in your messaging and there is clarity in
   communicating your full mission.

9. Board meetings are focused on culture, mission, and impact, and
   the board is aware of its role as guardians of the full mission.

10. You measure metrics capturing the entirety of your mission, not
    just inputs.

INTENTIONALITY

11. Prayer is fully integrated in decision making, in meeting struc-
    ture, and as a weekly or daily discipline for staff.

12. You have hiring practices that go beyond technical abilities and
    assess a candidate's full mission fit.

13. Prospective board members are interviewed by multiple board
    members and formally assessed for their personal faith and full
    missional alignment.

14. Compared to a year ago, staff and board members are showing
    increasing fruit in their lives (e.g., love, patience, kindness, etc.,
    Galatians 5:22–23) as evidence of the Holy Spirit at work in them.

15. There is a clearly articulated plan to create a culture that re-
    inforces your identity, and you have daily or weekly rituals that
    reinforce your organization's values and mission.

16. Church partnerships are a constant source of consideration for
    your organization.

17. If your leader suddenly left, you would not be concerned about
    the mission continuing.

18. A large percentage of your staff would leave the organization if
    you experienced Mission Drift.

19. You have said no to a "good opportunity" in the last two years
    because it did not fit with your identity and full mission.

20. You have a succession plan in place that is actively cultivating internal candidates for leadership, and there are known, potential future Mission True leaders.

Results: Score Intentionality and Clarity sections separately. Plotting yourself on the following grid, you will get some sense of whether your current practices are likely to result in Mission Drift or remaining Mission True:

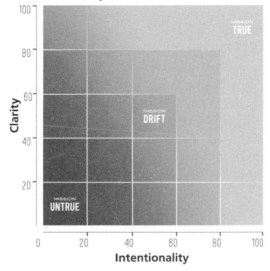

The closer you are to the top right, the more likely you are to withstand Mission Drift. Like a current, the closer you are to the bottom left, the greater the force pulling you toward secularism.

Movement is the one constant. It is always possible to fight against the current and move toward greater clarity of mission and intentionality of practices that help protect your mission. But if you don't make conscious efforts to fight against it, drift is inevitable.

Mission Untrue

In our research, we found there is a point of no return. A point when the flame of Christian distinctiveness loses all visibility. Despite their founding identity, they no longer have any concern about their Christian mission or any desire to create safeguards to protect it. Harvard, Yale, and ChildFund fit squarely in this category—Mission Untrue. They have no intention of returning to their roots. For these institutions, the train has departed the station. This might sound melodramatic—and maybe it is—but apart from a miraculous event, none of these institutions will recapture the Christian heritage of their youth. The interests opposing a return are strong and entrenched.

Christian distinctiveness no longer exists. Past leaders ignored or were indifferent to the causes of Mission Drift. And the current carried them to a point where they have a new mission, different values, and an altered DNA.

Derek Bok, president at Harvard University from 1971–1991, wrote a letter—one we will come back to later in the book—about Harvard's historical roots. After describing the journey Harvard walked over its history, Bok shared Harvard's current reality. "This is why particular religious doctrines, however important they may be in guiding the ethical beliefs of individual students, can never be adopted by a secular university."[8]

Harvard isn't a Christian faith-based organization any longer. This doesn't mean they aren't contributing in important ways to society. They are. But they have drifted beyond the tipping point, with no prospects of ever returning to the original vision of their founders.

At Harvard, ChildFund, and other Mission Untrue organizations, these markers are evidenced in changed mission statements, altered bylaws, and new names. These organizations have taken on a new identity. Agree or disagree with the new identity, there is no arguing they are no longer the organizations their founders intended.

Mission True

When Wess Stafford took the helm at Compassion International, he took the reins of an organization with tremendous clarity about its identity.

"I inherited from my three predecessors an organization centered on Christ and committed to being a servant to his bride, the church," Stafford commented.[9]

Compassion also safeguards their identity. They know they are susceptible to drift and devote money, prayer, and people to thinking about these issues every day. They reinforce their mission with the people they hire, the policies they set in motion, and the opportunities they pursue. Compassion is Mission True. Mission True organizations know who they are and actively safeguard, reinforce, and celebrate their DNA. Leaders constantly push toward higher levels of clarity about their mission and even more intentionality about protecting it.

"You can't just assume that a mission will take care of itself," stated Dr. Gene Habecker, president at Taylor University. "It will atrophy if you don't aggressively manage it in an ongoing way and continually reaffirm and integrate it into everything that you do over and over and over again. Mission management is never over. It's never done."[10]

Dr. Ben Sells, vice president of advancement at Taylor University, said it another way: "Our challenge going forward is to be more true to who we are than we've ever been before."[11]

These organizations know the DNA of their founders and replicate and reinforce that DNA in their organizations. They change and adapt, certainly, but they don't budge on mission. Their leaders are uniform on the immutables. They wake up thinking about their core identity and guard it with tenacious and contagious fervor.

"You take away the Gospel and you take the soul of our movement," shared Lisa Espineli Chinn, national director of international student ministry at InterVarsity. "Without the Gospel, what you have is a shell."[12]

This sentiment pervades Mission True organizations. They do not apologize for their Christian identity. They see their shared faith as an asset to their mission. It is what makes their organizations distinct in their industry and becomes the characteristic they celebrate more than any other.

The Gospel is not cursory within Mission True organizations. It is more than just a motivation. It is central. Everything else hinges around it.

Mission Drift

"Mission Drift is so slow you don't often see it," shared Terry Looper, business owner and board member at a number of faith-based organizations. "Consequently a lot of people don't really talk about it."

Again and again in our research, we saw how the second law of thermodynamics plays out within faith-based organizations: mission degenerates. Without generous doses of prayer and management, the gravitational current of secularization will have an unstoppable tug. Expansion, professionalization, and corporatization don't always dampen an organization's mission vibrancy, but they often do.

To avoid it, we must keep our eyes focused on protecting what matters most. Apathy or inactivity results in less clarity and less intentionality, and organizations awaken to the reality that they have drifted to the bottom left of the Mission Drift grid.

"I fear most Mission Drift is simply a failure of faithfulness," shared Dr. David Bronkema, chair of Eastern University's school of leadership and development. "I'm concerned many decisions that lead to drift are simply not prayerful decisions."[13]

It's almost as if Mission Drift just *happens to* organizations as they grow. Or at least that's what we heard Mission Drift leaders lamenting. But we don't think that has to be the case. Mission Drift is not inevitable.

When Christians forget that all we do flows out of our response to the undeserved grace we've experienced, we lack motivation and endurance. Professors Michael Barnett and Janice Gross Stein confirmed this in their book, *Sacred Aid*. Without faith, organizations lose their punch and lack the stamina to persevere through hardship.

Change is possible. Organizations in the midst of drift can reclaim their history and chart a comeback course. Dr. Mohler proved this, turning Southern Seminary from a drifting institution to a beacon of biblical faithfulness. It wasn't easy, but he illustrated an enduring principle: The best time to make difficult mission decisions is now.

Soon after taking the helm, Dr. Mohler wrote a letter to Southern Seminary's president 150 years in the future. He placed the letter in a time capsule and buried it on Southern's campus. While he didn't publicly disclose the letter, Dr. Mohler sent a signal when he put it into the ground: Southern Seminary was pouring its identity in cement. The letter made it clear that Southern's mission was no longer up for debate.

Through his actions, Mohler intensified the clarity of mission, the most pivotal aspect of Mission True organizations—*knowing who you are.*

Pain Avoidance

Matt Norman is a thought leader on business productivity and leadership. As president of Dale Carnegie North Central U.S., Norman coaches leaders and teams across the country. Norman often trains on the psychological state known as "pain avoidance."

In short, the biggest barrier leaders face in achieving success is their innate aversion to pain. We do the easy work first, ignoring the underlying and most complex challenges because we know it will hurt.

"The key to managing 'pain avoidance' begins with a clear and compelling vision of the future and follows with awareness that difficult choices get harder with time," Norman shared. "And, while it's tempting to delay these choices, normally we can realize the benefits sooner and minimize the pain to stakeholders if we act quickly."

Mission True leaders know painful decisions must be made. When Dr. Mohler arrived on Southern Seminary's campus, he found an organization with an identity crisis: *Which path would it take?* The beaten-down path many seminaries have taken toward cultural relevance was traveled by many forebearers. Leading Southern forward in this direction would have been less painful and probably met with less criticism.

The path to leading a Mission True organization is paved with hard decisions. The sooner leaders make those hard decisions, the higher the likelihood they will succeed and the less pain the organization will experience in the long haul.

But let there be no illusion: Just because leaders make decisions to return an organization to its founding principles does not mean they will be immune from pain. Mission True organizations often encounter pain *because of* their clarity about their mission.

The blows might be subtler. A corporate donor might decline your proposal because of your faith convictions. You might have to wait months or years longer to hire that key staff person because you are unflinching on hiring people who will carry forward the values and convictions of your organization.

The blows might be harsher. Remaining true to your mission or recapturing your founding values could collapse your organization. There might come a decision point when you are not capable of fulfilling your full mission and the only path forward demands you hang up the proverbial spikes. But how much better to collapse in allegiance than to survive by compromising on what matters most?

The best organizations don't mourn this pain. They acknowledge the difficulty, but they do not lament it happened. Like the physical burn of a great workout, they understand this discomfort will only forge their resolve. As James, the brother of Jesus, wrote, "Consider it pure joy, my brothers and sisters, whenever you face trials of many kinds, because you know that the testing of your faith produces perseverance."[14]

Mission True Decision Making

Mission True organizations take active steps in staying Mission True. Mission True organizations:

1. *Seek clarity first.* Having mission clarity is like mapping your destination. Having an end point helps you communicate your route—your culture, hiring practices—to reach your journey's end. Whether or not others agree, they know where you stand. Individuals can join you for the entire journey, find areas of common ground to ride with you for part of the trip, or amicably find another path.

2. *Acknowledge that the pressure to drift is a constant.* Without intentionality in small decisions, mission creep occurs, even with people fanatic about the mission. Employees must live and breathe the mission daily.

3. *Realize there's a point of no return.* Organizations like Harvard and the Y have drifted so far that their identity has transformed; they have become what we call Mission Untrue. No ministry or organization is exempt from this course, no matter how central an organization's Christian identity is.

4. *Make hard decisions to correct drift.* If an organization is drifting far from its initial purpose, then God can empower leaders to turn it around, but it often requires drastic measures. Pain avoidance is the fastest way for Mission Drift to devastate an organization's Christ-centered identity.

The more we learned about Mission True organizations, the more excited we became. These organizations understood how to identify drift and then how to protect against it. But their practices aren't new.

We found these very practices instituted by a leader nearly one hundred years ago. He was a trailblazing Mission True leader, and he taught us a number of foundational lessons about Mission Drift. Sometimes you find innovation in surprising places. And we found his story on the back of a cereal box.

5

THE SECRET RECIPE TO QUAKER OATS

Mission True leaders assume they will face
drift and build safeguards against it

Trademark Generosity

Henry Crowell was not an alpha CEO. He was not an "all-eyes-on-me" sort of leader. Instead, he was thoughtful, quiet. But that made the words and actions of the founder of Quaker Oats Company all the more meaningful. His resolve enabled him to succeed in business.

His chief business accomplishment was purchasing and turning around the Quaker Mill, in Ravenna, Ohio, from bankruptcy[1] to a $250 million business in his lifetime.[2] His quiet strength not only made Crowell formidable in business, but also a trailblazer in championing causes of justice.

Crowell and his wife, Susan Coleman Crowell, helped rid Chicago of its Red Light District, which had over a thousand brothels in the early 1900s. Crowell served with a group of business and civic leaders on the "Committee of Fifteen," and together they led a relentless campaign against the promoters of the prostitution racket in the city. By 1935, almost all were shut down, and the prominent supporters of the trade had vacated the city.[3]

Howard Haylett served alongside Henry Crowell for many years as the director of the Committee of Fifteen. He said:

> I tell you, Mr. Crowell was a power for righteousness in Chicago. It was not his money, although he gave thousands. It was himself. He always came to Committee meetings. During the sessions, he sat quietly, his hands folded on the table. As we were about to adjourn, someone would say, "What do you think we should do, Mr. Crowell?" He quietly told us. We did it.[4]

A long bout with life-threatening tuberculosis in Henry Crowell's youth—the same sickness that took the lives of his grandfather, father, and two brothers—forged his resolve. The health battles strengthened his character. Preparing him for a life of leadership, his suffering also made Crowell self-deprecating and selfless.

Of the many businesses Crowell started, the Quaker Oats Company is the most prominent. With Crowell at the helm, Quaker Oats pioneered an approach to marketing that separated it from the competitors. From painted advertisements on the outside of train cars to the iconic Quaker logo—the world's first registered trademark for a cereal—Crowell deployed his considerable business savvy to take his company to the top of its industry.

Drift Concerns

Though he had business success, he was equally renowned for his openhandedness. After his near-death experience as a teenager, Crowell made a commitment to generosity. And as he began to amass a fortune, easily one of the wealthiest people in his generation, Crowell's conviction about generosity only increased. For more than forty years, Crowell gave away over 70 percent of his income.

A friend once asked Crowell how much he gave, in sum, toward charity.

He responded, "Well, I've never even let myself in on that."[5]

The preeminent motivator of Crowell's generosity was the advancement of evangelical Christianity. He was unwavering in his commitment to the Gospel and to the authority of God's Word. One of his closest friends and allies in ministry was Dwight L. Moody, the evangelist who would go on to found Moody Bible Institute. Crowell funded a number of ministries connected to Moody and served as chairman of the board at Moody Bible Institute for over forty years.

Though not a natural cynic, Crowell grew weary of the Mission Drift surfacing around him. When his own church and denomination began to employ pastors who denied the authority of God's Word, questioning the truths Christians had believed for centuries, Crowell began a long process of attempting to turn the ship back toward orthodoxy.

But in the end, the denomination had moved past the point of no return. Crowell was firm, yet conciliatory, in his departing letter to the leaders of his denomination.

> The appeal of Modernism appears to be gaining strength . . . the denomination is standing on dangerous ground . . . something should be done at once to stop this drift toward Modernism and I have thought of nothing better than for me to withdraw from the church as a definite force protest against changing standards and the weakening of the church's loyalty and devotion to Jesus Christ.[6]

The Crowell Trust Is Born

When he saw his very own church slip into secularism, Crowell developed a sobering realization about his own wealth: It might not go where he wanted it to after he died. He determined to do something to prevent that from happening. In the same way Crowell deployed his creativity toward leading his business, he innovated in the way he gave and safeguarded his future giving: "I want the rest of it to go to the work of the Lord Christ Jesus. But I desire that it be protected from the wiles of evil ones, who are much interested in the loaves and fishes, but not at all in the faith."[7]

In other words, Crowell knew that, unguarded, his wealth would be disbursed to a number of worthy causes, but not toward the cause he cared about the most: Jesus. So, he created a trust where the income "would be appropriated from time to time to such institutions only as are loyal to the [Christian] Faith."[8]

Crowell guarded the Trust with a group of five trustees, members chosen after a long and thorough vetting process. He chose them each carefully, knowing whims and agendas could easily supplant the work he intended with his funds.

Crowell also safeguarded his trust against drifting charities. For example, Crowell required charities to make funding requests annually.

This, he felt, was an easy way to protect against drift: "If any beneficiary evidences a drift toward Modernism—then, no more appropriation."[9]

Since its founding, The Crowell Trust has journeyed through multiple world wars, the invention of mobile phones, and over a dozen different American presidents. The times and mediums have changed, yet Crowell's heartbeat pulses the same. The trustees today work from the same charter, on the same mission, with the same priorities as Henry Crowell. Each year, the Trust distributes millions of dollars to evangelical Christian ministries across the globe.

Once a year, the trustees gather to observe a rather particular tradition written in The Crowell Trust's charter: First, they begin in prayer. Next, they read—aloud—the mission and vision Henry Crowell himself wrote. They read his words and meditate on the vision God gave him before starting official foundation business.

From the outside looking in, the tradition seems almost comical: a group of high-powered executive leaders sitting for three hours while reading aloud to one another. But it is a practice demonstrating a defining characteristic of Mission True organizations: They proactively protect their mission, understanding that every organization is susceptible to drift.

"Many folks come into the Crowell Trust and tell me that Crowell is one of the few trusts that have stayed true to its indenture," noted Candy Sparks, current executive director of The Crowell Trust. "Our mission is the teaching and active extension of evangelical Christianity. This statement guides the staff and the trustees, helping us to keep on task."[10]

Abolitionists and Oil Tycoons

John Howard Pew was just a child when Henry Crowell launched Quaker Oats. Though much younger, he mirrored Crowell's fervor for entrepreneurship and for the Gospel. He built his empire selling oil, not oatmeal, serving most of his career as the president of Sunoco (known then as Sun Oil).

The Pew family was known for being devoutly Christian.[11] They were compelled by their Christian faith to advance abolition and became a strong force against slavery in the United States. The Pews were known widely for their evangelical convictions and commitment to justice.

Howard Pew carried the family mantle into his career. After graduating from Grove City College, Howard went to work for his father at Sunoco and climbed his way up to the chief executive role. After he retired from the company, he continued to influence it as a member of the board, and later as the board's chairman. Under Pew's leadership, Sunoco grew nearly forty times over.

During this time, Pew became an outspoken and generous philanthropist. A devout Presbyterian, he believed Christ was the only true hope for the world. Together with four of his siblings, Howard founded the Pew Memorial Foundation, which eventually became an umbrella foundation over seven trusts in the Pew name, known today as the Pew Charitable Trusts.[12]

The five siblings, headed by Howard Pew, worked hard to decide who would be the beneficiaries of the family's fortune, and "they approved all grants at regular meetings and most of their gifts had a personal connection."[13] Like The Crowell Trust, the Pew Charitable Trusts avoided automatically renewing grants to ensure organizations remained faithful to the Gospel. Like The Crowell Trust, "they gave one-year grants."[14]

The Pew family cared about advancing the Gospel. This priority was clearly reflected in their giving. In the Pew Charitable Trusts' infancy, they made extraordinarily generous donations to organizations committed to Christian principles.

Contributions from the Pews fueled the growth of many prominent Christian institutions, such as Grove City College in Pennsylvania—

where the Fine Arts Building still bears Howard's name. They also gave generously to Fuller Theological Seminary and Moody Bible Institute, the same organization Henry Crowell propelled in the university's earliest days.

As his prominence grew, Pew met a fiery young man with an insatiable hunger for telling others about Jesus. Like Crowell with Moody, Pew was smitten by the fire in the belly of the young preacher. The preacher knew nothing about oil, but he knew how to preach, and with Pew's help, Billy Graham shared the Gospel with more people than perhaps any other person in the history of the world.

A Street Preacher and an Oilman

Billy Graham was a risk-taker. And so was Howard Pew. Which is what made their partnership work.

In 1955, Graham sat down with Pew in his Sunoco headquarters. While Pew puffed on a cigar, Graham laid out his vision for a magazine of "evangelical conviction." Graham envisioned the magazine "would restore intellectual respectability and spiritual impact to evangelical Christianity; it would reaffirm the power of the Word of God to redeem and transform men and women."

Graham shared his vision passionately and concluded his pitch with a bold question to Pew.

"Would you contribute heavily to that?"

Pew took in the question slowly, pulling deeply on his cigar. He gazed out on Walnut Street through his office window, taking in the towering skyscrapers fronting the storied Philadelphia thoroughfare. His confidence in Graham—and his idea—grew while he paused.

"I think we can do it," Pew responded.

And they did it. This historic meeting led to the launch of *Christianity Today*, now reaching over 2.5 million people monthly through their global brands. Pew gave $150,000 to launch the evangelical magazine.[15] Though Graham had the vision for the magazine, he knew he couldn't do it alone. "Without [Howard's] support I have no doubt the project would have failed," Graham shared.

That meeting started an exciting and historically significant friendship between Pew and Graham. This friendship, galvanized by their
shared conviction for advancement of the Gospel, wasn't just a social
connection. They were partners and builders, and an unlikely pair at
that: a Presbyterian oil magnate and a farm-boy-turned-evangelist.
The duo accomplished much together, and Graham held great esteem
for Pew.

"I came to have great affection and admiration for him," Graham
said, "not because he had a great deal of money but because he was
a man of God and a man of wisdom who wanted to see his wealth
used wisely for the cause of Christ."[16]

Howard Pew died in 1971. Graham spoke at Pew's funeral. The
Pew Charitable Trusts paid homage to Pew's friendship with Graham,
donating $3 million toward the construction of the Billy Graham
Memorial Library.[17]

Planned Parenthood and Raging Incrementalism

Unfortunately, since the founders died, the Pew Charitable Trusts
have provided another example of Mission Drift. And it's received
significant public scrutiny because of its departure from Howard Pew's
intentions.

The drift has been so marked that one author described it as "the
gravest violation of donor intent."[18] In other words, the Pew Charitable
Trusts hasn't done what Howard Pew founded it to do. But it's more
than inadvertent creep. In many ways, they've taken a full U-turn from
the work he believed in.

In recent years, the Pew Charitable Trusts have made major gifts to
organizations like Planned Parenthood and many of the Ivy League
schools Howard Pew eschewed. In a revealing article in the *Philadelphia Inquirer* about the shifting priorities at the Pew Charitable Trusts,
journalist Lucinda Fleeson noted the stark change.

[Howard] Pew couldn't find any seminary conservative enough . . .
so he built his own. In 1970 he bought a 100-acre former Carmelite
monastery near Boston and created the Gordon-Conwell Theological

Seminary to turn out the type of ministers he sought. He built much of the campus and promised yearly checks to keep it operating. Today, the Pew Charitable Trusts give millions of dollars to Princeton University and other Ivy League colleges. They have cut off the annual funding to the Gordon-Conwell seminary.[19]

Fleeson noted the change in giving philosophy as well. In the early years of the Pew Charitable Trusts, Howard and his siblings insisted on abiding by the biblical teachings about generosity, modeling humility in the ways they gave. But today, the Trust has gone to the other side of the spectrum. "Instead of quiet anonymity, Pew's professional managers are seeking a national identity and name recognition for Pew comparable to those of America's other great foundations."[20]

Scarcely a Resemblance

The last Pew to serve on the Pew Charitable Trusts board who shared Howard Pew's convictions was his cousin, Jack Pew. Advocating for a mission that remained true to Howard Pew's convictions, Jack found himself consistently outvoted at Pew board meetings. He was forced to resign.

"I just don't like the way those people do business," Jack shared with colleagues upon his departure.[21]

In response to criticism of its drift, Rebecca Rimel, current president and CEO of the Pew Charitable Trusts, said, "[Howard] was a man of strong convictions and his successors on our board are following in his tradition by having strong convictions."[22]

But strong convictions, in themselves, mean little if they stand in sharp contrast to the beliefs of the founders who created the hundreds of millions of dollars Rimel and the current trustees give away.

The drastic changes in the philosophy, staff, trustees, and values of the Pew Trusts are unnerving. How could a foundation built by Howard Pew—a lifelong ministry partner with Billy Graham and adamant proponent of evangelical Christianity—drift so far in such a short amount of time?

Safeguarding Mission

Henry Crowell and Howard Pew shared much in common. Both identified first as Christians. Both were titans in their industries, Crowell
in food, Pew in oil. Both were extraordinarily generous. But what
distinguishes the legacy of their charitable trusts is safeguards.

Henry Crowell attended to the details. He placed guardrails around
the vision and funds God entrusted to him. Howard Pew's successors
took his intent and replaced it with their own. Exploiting loopholes in
the bylaws, they pushed their own agendas, funding the very institutions Pew spoke out against.

The Pew Charitable Trusts today fund many admirable causes. They
continue to donate toward projects in partnership with *Christianity
Today* and have commissioned significant research at the intersection
of culture, religion, and politics. And they fund some of our favorite
radio programs! But their priorities bear little resemblance to the
convictions and legacy of Howard Pew and his predecessors. The
problem isn't the mission of the Pew Charitable Trusts today. The
problem is with the blunt change of course.

It is the responsibility of leaders to remain faithful in safeguarding
the mission of their organizations. We do not believe in uniformity of
mission, as if only certain flavors of organizations are approved by
God. As Paul compellingly asked, "If all were a single member, where
would the body be? As it is, there are many parts, yet one body."[23] The
world needs the Church engaging faithfully in all areas of culture.
And this will demand many varieties of organizations.

Whatever the specific purpose, however, let's be intentional in defining and protecting it. In the journey toward remaining Mission
True, safeguards matter.

Causes and Safeguards

Thus far, we have examined the histories of storied organizations like
Harvard, Yale, ChildFund, and the Pew Trusts. These organizations
are Mission Untrue. They are not the organizations their founders
envisioned. They have shifted courses in dramatic ways, taking on
entirely new identities as they have grown and aged.

The more we learned about their organizations, the more we recognized how significant our donor conversation in the Houston boardroom was to the future of HOPE International. If we didn't identify how these organizations drifted, we might find our organization drifting in the same current, toward a watered-down and secularized identity. Was it just a matter of time till we succumbed to Mission Drift?

Compassion and the Crowell Trust gave us hope. We believe their stories—along with the many others we profile in the remainder of this book—will inspire you as they did us. Mission Drift is not inevitable.

Mission True Safeguards

Protecting our Christian distinctiveness will not be easy, but it will always be worth it. The Gospel is what our world most needs us to protect. Mission True organizations:

1. *Remain mindful of cultural trends.* Henry Crowell recognized the cultural shift away from orthodoxy that would only be amplified with time. His foresight led to the Crowell Trust remaining true. Sensitive to the cultural climate, Mission True organizations have the wisdom to build guardrails.

2. *Don't assume successors will inherit the founder's vision.* Unlike Crowell, Howard Pew believed his successors would defend his values, which led to drift. Mission True organizations intentionally train and educate the next generation, a subject we cover more extensively in chapter 9.

3. *Attend to the details in constructing safeguards.* Crowell advocated for simple practices that now outlive him. Clearly defining his intent in writing, as well as having the board read the charter aloud each year, helped enable Crowell's vision to flourish today.

We learned a lot about how drift happens and how we can protect against it. Mission True organizations—across all different sectors— mirrored each other in the ways they safeguarded against it. These qualities enveloped all facets of faith-based organizations.

Mission True organizations understand that remaining true means they must think about Mission Drift in their boards, leaders, staffs, donors, metrics, programs, organizational culture, language, and their commitment to working with the church. Organizations drift when they underestimate the importance of any of these areas. Mission True organizations believe that throwing up our arms and floating in the strong currents of Mission Drift is not an option. Remaining on course won't be easy, but we will not regret it.

6

You Know Why You Exist

Mission True organizations have clarity about their mission

What's in a Name?

London was a place of cultural upheaval and dramatic social change in the early 1800s. William Wilberforce famously led the courageous fight against the slave trade—we'll come back to this story later. But while he was delivering compelling speeches to bureaucrats in the House of Commons, a different battle raged in the gritty streets of inner-city London.

George Williams, a young boy when Wilberforce's efforts ended the slave trade, had compassion on youth in the London slums. They had come to London for work, but many had fallen into crime.

So Williams started a Bible study for displaced young men in 1844, which became a movement later known as the Young Men's Christian Association (YMCA). As its name indicated, Christ was at its core.

Williams said, "Our object is the improvement of the spiritual condition of the young men engaged in houses of business, by the formation of Bible classes, family and social prayer meetings, mutual improvement societies, or any other spiritual agency."[1]

Its founding motto came from Jesus' prayer "that they all may be one; as thou, Father, art in me, and I in thee, that they also may be one in us: that the world may believe that thou has sent me."[2] On the south side of the Westminster Abbey sanctuary, a beautiful stained glass commemorates Williams and the YMCA for their remarkable work.[3]

The YMCA Goes West

The YMCA spread across the ocean and took off in the United States. Its early champions include the great evangelist Dwight L. Moody, founder of Moody Bible Institute, who was the president of the Chicago YMCA.[4] But it was under the leadership of John Mott, who started working for YMCA in 1888, that its foreign missionary arm, the Student Volunteer Movement, became "one of the most successful missionary-recruiting organizations of all time."[5]

Helping generate interest in missions and providing training, the YMCA directly and indirectly commissioned over 20,000 missionaries.[6]

Mott's most popular book, *The Evangelization of the World in This Generation*, shared about the dedicated, passionate young people giving themselves to the Gospel. It was the slogan of the era. And Mott won a Nobel Prize.

But something soon changed. Disillusioned by the Great War, young people started to become skeptical of Christianity and began to lose their faith. A fissure began to grow within the Church between those who argued the preeminence of words and those who argued the preeminence of deeds.

With revenue declining, the YMCA decided to emphasize its fitness programs and downplay its biblical training. During the 1970s and 1980s, the YMCA reinvented itself: It became a family fitness center. I (Peter) enjoy playing racquetball at the YMCA with my family, and it's still a great institution, but it is not fulfilling its original purpose. Funding pressures, bad leadership decisions, and poor mission management gave way to a changing of the "why."

When we began our research, the YMCA featured George Williams's story prominently on their web site. The lengthy profile documented Williams's fervent Christian faith and his driving passion to introduce young boys in London to Jesus Christ. Today, however, leaders at the YMCA have sanitized the story. They even changed their name to match their new identity.

In 2010, the YMCA had dropped everything but the "Y."[7]

More British Bible Studies

"There are a lot of universities trying to derecognize us," Alec Hill, president of InterVarsity USA, shared calmly. "But we have a Lord we have to obey."[8]

Just a few decades after George Williams started Bible studies and prayer meetings with London's street youth, a group of British students founded InterVarsity at the University of Cambridge in 1877. These bold students prayed, studied the Bible, and shared their faith with their classmates, despite the harsh disapproval of university officials. Over 130 years later, InterVarsity stands Mission True.

InterVarsity now serves students on nearly six hundred campuses, their leaders' hearts beating to the same cadence as the students who founded InterVarsity. But like the first InterVarsity group, they face increasing pressures on campuses across the country.

Over the past few years, news outlets like the *Wall Street Journal* featured the stories, all with the same basic headline: *Christian organization expelled from campus*. Officials at over fifty universities— including prominent colleges like Rutgers, Georgetown, Vanderbilt, and the University of Michigan—have challenged InterVarsity's right to be a registered student organization.

On a handful of campuses, school officials have given InterVarsity the proverbial pink slip. Because InterVarsity requires their student leaders to be Christians, these schools allege "religious discrimination." Vanderbilt hit national news in 2012 when university officials voted to disallow the organization on campus.

Nicholas Zappos, Vanderbilt's chancellor, outlined the university's position:

We . . . require all Vanderbilt registered student organizations to observe our nondiscrimination policy. That means membership in registered student organizations is open to everyone and that everyone, if desired, has the opportunity to seek leadership positions.[9]

In short, Zappos believes a Christian ministry restricting leadership to Christians is impermissible. And the implications of this rationale extend far beyond university campuses. The implications extend to foundations, urban ministries, and missions agencies. And it is in these moments when leaders of faith-based organizations face two options.

The first option? "You can kowtow to the pressure," Hill shared, "accommodating culture to be liked and accepted."

Or you can stand by your convictions, knowing it could hurt. Hill and InterVarsity's leaders didn't back down. They doubled down, refusing to bend their knee to those who demanded they change their mission or soften their approach. Softening their approach, they realize, would strip away their very *raison d'être*—their reason for existing.

InterVarsity student leaders at the University at Buffalo of the State University of New York understood the significance of their crossroads when officials asked them to change their club's constitution to open leadership to everyone. These courageous students knew the stakes were high. They knew their immutables and didn't budge on their core.

The students resolved to retain their constitution.[10]

It's more than keeping a constitution. InterVarsity leaders decided to retain their identity.

"Holding the Gospel in humility and grace," Hill responded. "We will . . . act within our rights to be faithful to our calling."[11]

Focusing on the Why

The Y and InterVarsity—two grassroots organizations created to share God's Word and encourage prayer among British youth. Both grew and expanded across the globe. And both serve a unique purpose today. But one—the Y—looks nothing like the organization George Williams founded. The other, InterVarsity, carries the same DNA it had in the beginning.

We believe the Y had an ordering problem. They changed with the currents of culture, adapting and morphing on their core. They are Mission Untrue. They bent on their immutables. In contrast, Inter-Varsity changed as it grew and expanded, but it never changed the things that matter most. It didn't shift on its core identity and mission. Mission True organizations ask different questions.

Leaders often first ask *what*, then move to *how*, and finally transition to *why*. That's a natural progression. But great innovators, according to Simon Sinek, a globally renowned consultant and author, start with *why*.[12] This leads to *how* and, finally, *what*. The ordering really matters.

For example, a traditional computer company strategy goes like this:

- What? We make great computers.
- How? They're beautifully designed and simple to use.
- Why? Want to buy one?[13]

Sinek recognized that people are not motivated to buy or join a movement because they need a product. Rather, they must *believe* in the company. If they don't know the why, the company can be easily replaced and can quickly lose its way.

He uses the example of Apple, which asks its questions in reverse:

- Why? We believe in challenging the status quo. We believe in thinking differently.
- How? We make beautifully designed and simple-to-use products.
- What? We just happen to make great computers—want to buy one?[14]

Apple's decision to prioritize *why* led to customer loyalty. Whether they make phones or computers doesn't matter. People are sold on their identity, not just the product. Other companies are just as equipped to create quality products. But customers want to believe in the company.[15]

Everything flows from *why*. Not only does it motivate others to join you, it also guides what you do—and often more important—what you *don't* do. Having clarity on your purpose prevents the types of changes evidenced by the Y.

"The single greatest reason for Mission Drift is the lack of a clear mission and vision," reflected David Wills, president of National Christian Foundation. "Crystal clear vision is the starting point for avoiding Mission Drift. . . . If you don't know where you are going, any road will get you there."[16]

Your company could bring in the greatest inventors to produce ideas. Many of these ideas could be very good. But you must return to the *why*—do the ideas align with your purpose?

Mission True organizations distinguish between guarding the mission and guarding the means. Knowing who you are is the first line of defense against drift; it allows you to determine if change and adjustments are equipping you to better accomplish your mission or slowly moving you away from your foundation.

This is what InterVarsity understood. They knew their why.

Modern-Day Barbershop Quartets

Young Life also models this principle beautifully. Their mission—their *why*—is to point young people to Jesus. Because they work with teenagers—a demographic known for rapid change—they need to remain young, even as they age.

"If we lose touch with one generation of teenagers," said Young Life's Marty Caldwell, "we'll be completely ineffective in about eight years."[17]

In the early days Young Life ministered to high school students with evangelistic barbershop quartets. Men in pinstripes singing in four-part harmony wouldn't capture the imaginations of today's teenagers. Instead Young Life has taken to cell phones and social media.

But they haven't forgotten the *why*: today they still proclaim Christ to students. Though their methods have changed, they continue to stay with their core purpose.

Grounded in *why*, Young Life is free to live out its mission without clinging to its *how*.

Not all change is drift. Jesus' ministry looked different depending on the audience and culture. His approach to the Samaritan woman differed from His approach to the Pharisees. His method looked different with the rich young ruler than it did with Zacchaeus. Jesus understood His why. His purpose. And His means of reaching them were as varied as the people themselves: parables, healings, miracles, chastisements, prophetic warnings, blessings, and curses.

Our means should be just as varied. Only when we understand why our organizations exist—who we are—can we begin to safeguard ourselves from Mission Drift. And then we can begin to differentiate between change and drift.

As Young Life demonstrates, knowing *why* you exist creates the right filter for change. Knowing this allows you to define your immutables. All the tactical "what" decisions flow out of that. And that might mean you change your core methodology, as evidenced by a Fortune 100 company in the Wild West.

In the Stagecoach Business?

Stagecoaches used to be the lifeblood of the Wild West. In the times of the California Gold Rush and the decades afterward, stagecoaches were the most reliable way to travel and transport goods from the East to the West.

In 1859, stagecoach express mail was the one reliable way to send letters and gold across the vast American deserts and mountains. One company had a reputation as the most reliable stagecoach company in the Wild West, but their leaders always knew they weren't a stagecoach company. And knew they weren't even a transportation company. To connect people and protect and transport their most valuable possessions—this was why they existed.

For stagecoach operations, there was an imminent threat of highwaymen and bandits, but by the end of the 1800s, a much bigger foe had appeared and ushered in a new era: the railway. As the railways expanded, the stagecoach business lost its preeminent role as the bridge between the East and the West.

Stagecoach companies began collapsing across the country. But this one company—Wells Fargo & Co.—outlasted the rest. It stayed afloat by refocusing on its ability to connect people, money, and goods. Wells Fargo eventually left the transportation industry entirely to become the Fortune 100 banking giant it is today.

As bankrupted stagecoach companies began to dot the western plains, Wells Fargo flourished. It thrived because its leaders knew why the company existed. Today, Wells Fargo still boasts a stagecoach in its company logo, but it would no longer be in business if Wells Fargo's leaders had lost sight of their core mission.

When Churches Look Like Culture

It's hard to imagine a church forgetting why it exists, but in the United States, we've seen how churches can lose their way. Their missions have grown cloudy.

One denomination reported losing nearly 25 percent of its congregants in the last few decades.[18] Another lost over 10 percent in two years alone.[19] Many mainline denominations mirror this fate. When I (Chris) was searching for a church a few years ago, I visited all the churches within walking distance of my house. I frequented many mainline churches throughout my neighborhood. They shared a few characteristics: Their congregations were aging, and their beautiful historic buildings were nearly empty.

The decline centers not around programs or worship styles, but because they have forgotten why they exist. Forgetting their mission, they have slowly drifted to look largely like the culture surrounding them.

"Study after study has shown that religions that grow are the ones that are hard-core in some way. They have something that differs sharply from the culture in which they operate," says Boston University professor of religion Stephen Prothero. "That's the problem with mainline Protestantism: It's not different enough from mainstream America."[20]

The pressures of Mission Drift are strong. And it is not surprising to see churches and denominations abandon the truth of the Gospel as they age. Perhaps part of the problem is that we've forgotten that our churches need to be distinct. Jesus was clear on this.

You are the salt of the earth, but if salt has lost its taste, how shall its saltiness be restored? It is no longer good for anything except to be thrown out and trampled under people's feet.

You are the light of the world. A city set on a hill cannot be hidden. Nor do people light a lamp and put it under a basket, but on a stand, and it gives light to all in the house. In the same way, let your light shine before others, so that they may see your good works and give glory to your Father who is in heaven.[21]

Many churches and denominations have lost their saltiness. They have forgotten why they exist and have moved away from a core commitment to the Gospel. Today, they resemble little more than a country club without a golf course. And so their light dims and their pews sit empty.

Change ≠ Drift

While it's easy to label all changes as drift, sometimes change is necessary to stay on mission. Being Mission True isn't synonymous with being unchanging. On the contrary, remaining Mission True will demand you change to continue to fulfill your mission. When the YMCA and ChildFund changed their names, it was symbolic of their new identities. They both took the word *Christian* out.

Another organization did nearly the same. And when the world's largest Christ-centered nonprofit[22] takes "Christ" out of its name, it's worth examining. When Campus Crusade for Christ changed its name to Cru in 2012, the world noticed. And reacted . . . strongly.

Donors, newscasters, and talk show hosts lambasted the organization. Critics suggested Cru was rolling down the "slippery slope" toward spiritual apathy. They saw the change and assumed it meant Cru was following the path of many before it—downplaying its Christian distinction and soft-pedaling its faith convictions. But Cru leaders believe just the opposite is true.

"We didn't start off and say, 'Let's take Christ out of the name,'" Steve Sellers, vice president of the U.S. Campus Crusade for Christ, told ABC News. "That's kind of where the firestorm has come. People are making it look like we're bowing to political correctness, but that was absolutely never even a discussion point."[23]

At first glance, Cru's decision looks like ChildFund, an instance where the name change verbalized the shifting identity. But for Cru, the founding mission was the *driver* behind the name change. Retiring their previous name allowed them to live out their mission.

"Campus Crusade" may not be offensive to those raised in the church subculture, but those aren't the people Bill Bright hoped to reach with the Gospel. When he founded Campus Crusade in 1951, he sensed God stirring him to introduce unchurched college students to the person of Jesus Christ. That was his *why*.

And for many decades, Campus Crusade was the right name for that ministry. But, over time, their name became an inhibitor, not an accelerator, of Bill Bright's vision. On the name change, Cru leaders explained:

> Our name presented obstacles to our mission. . . . The word "cru-sade"—while common and acceptable in 1951 when we were founded—now carries negative associations. It acts as a barrier to the very people that we want to connect with. . . . Our surveys show that, in the U.S., twenty percent of the people willing to consider the gospel are less interested in talking with us after they hear the name. We are changing the name for the sake of more effective ministry.[24]

When it discovered that its original name was impeding them from reaching 20 percent of their target audience, Campus Crusade's leaders made the difficult decision to change its name. Its new name, Cru, provides an opportunity for its leaders to better fulfill their mission. It was a bold move, but it was a Mission True decision, opening doors for their mission in ways their previous name did not.

For the sake of our founding identities, we must be willing to make hard decisions. Cru did. And though some didn't like the change, many Christian leaders rose to their defense.

"Recently there has been much talk in ministry circles concerning the new name for Campus Crusade for Christ," shared Louie Giglio, founder and pastor of Passion Conferences and Passion City Church. "Though the organization's name has changed, its heartbeat remains the same . . . namely the mission of taking the name of Jesus to every person on the planet."[25]

Mission True Organizations

The "Y" betrayed its "why." It took on many new "why's" as it grew and professionalized, but its identity has been in constant motion since its founding. Staying Mission True means you know the *why*: What is your purpose? Mission True organizations answer this question with consistency over time. Mission True Organizations:

1. *Know why they exist*: They are students of their organizational history and can clearly articulate the organization's reason for existing.
2. *Differentiate means from mission*: They understand what is immutable and what is not. They know where they are willing to budge and where they won't.
3. *Change to reinforce their core mission*: They are not stagnant. They do not avoid change; instead they pursue change when it will help them become more true to their values and purpose.

Leaders at InterVarsity, Young Life, and Cru understand this. Recognizing their susceptibility to drift, they are unswerving in their conviction about their identity. They change and adapt, but they do not touch their immutables. Their core remains true.

Andy Stanley, senior pastor of North Point Community Church in Alpharetta, Georgia, cuts straight to the heart of the difference between change and drift when he writes, "Be stubborn about the vision. Be flexible with your plan. Strategies and timelines are always up for grabs."[26]

Mission True organizations start with a clear definition of their purpose. Nurturing, clarifying, and defending this purpose is the chief responsibility of those in the board room. It is their most sacred task.

Since publishing *Mission Drift* in early 2014, we have been encouraged and inspired by the work of a courageous and growing cohort of YMCA leaders from across the United States who are committed to seeing the YMCA reclaim its full mission. What's more, this group is supported by a number of prominent YMCA chapters that have never drifted from the founding mission of the YMCA. These leaders and chapters are joined by many YMCA programs around the world that have remained holistic and resolute in cultivating their Christ-centered mission.

7

Guardians
of the Mission

Mission True board members
understand their top priority

Red-Circled Letters

Mary Smith[1] opened the envelope nervously. Glancing at the return address, she knew what the envelope contained. As she opened it, she saw her organization's newsletter, riddled with red ink.

As president of a faith-based agricultural agency, Smith had received more than a few similar envelopes from this particular board member. And every time it was the same: This board member was unhappy that the organization continued to talk about Jesus.

Why do you keep muddying the waters with the faith stuff?

In the newsletters he mailed back to Smith, he used stark red ink to circle all mentions of faith, God, church, and Jesus. He wanted it gone.

As president, Smith reported to her board. They were her bosses. They hired her. And they had the power to fire her. When a board member sends any piece of mail, it's notable. When it's clear the board member is unhappy, it creates stomach ulcers.

Then came the phone call from the board member. He reiterated his argument. The organization was in the environmental industry, not the faith business. The board member attended church. He wasn't anti-Christian. He was just committed to helping this organization be all they could be.

With their continued emphasis on faith, he felt they limited their donor pool, capped their ability to recruit talented staff, and diverted their attention from the *real* work.

Smith faced a serious dilemma.

Keepers of the Mission

"It's the board," stated Al Mueller without hesitation. "It's all about the board. Everything hinges on them."[2]

As CEO at Excellence in Giving, a philanthropic advisory firm, Mueller advises high-capacity donors and organizations they support. And for him, Mission Drift starts and ends with the men and women sitting on the board.

They set policy, guide strategy, and manage the senior executive. They govern the organization. But even more, they protect the mission. Board members are guardians.

"Boards of faith-based organizations are often filled with well-meaning people," shared Lowell Haines, a lawyer, board member at Taylor University, and consultant to many other boards. "But most boards don't realize it is their fiduciary duty to remain loyal to the mission of their organizations. . . . This is the law."[3]

Serving on a board isn't akin to sitting on a donor club. It's not just a buddy circle for the organization's founder or president. Serving on a board is an important position. An organization cannot remain true to its mission without a diligent and protective board.

The Governance Dance

Mary Smith considered her options carefully as she thought about the confrontations with her irritated board member. She reported to the board. But Smith also disagreed with his position. As president, she couldn't just roll over and acquiesce to the board member's complaints. It was her organization's Christian distinctiveness she valued most.

"In some ways we emphasized the spiritual outreach as a reaction to seeing people become more prosperous," shared Smith. Their program was working. People were escaping material poverty. "But we would see their lives fall apart *because of* their prosperity. . . . First they purchase a TV, then buy more alcohol, and finally they can afford a mistress. . . . I'm still old-fashioned enough to believe that a man can gain the whole world and still forfeit his soul."

Smith believes financial prosperity isn't enough. In fact, financial prosperity can create hosts of new problems—alcoholism, materialism, and isolation.

This organization wasn't created to be an excellent secular agricultural agency. It was founded with a clear Christian identity. To sideline this distinction would cut to the organization's very reason for existence.

Rather than acquiesce to the board member's request, Smith sounded the alarm.

Calling some of the other board members, she shared about the marked-up newsletters and the related phone calls. The other board members agreed with Smith. The Christian distinction was at the core of their mission. They wouldn't budge.

Thankfully, they avoided nasty boardroom showdowns. With a clear majority in favor of protecting the organization's unique identity, they safeguarded the mission. The frustrated board member reached the end of his term. He was not renewed.

Three Cups of Nepotism

Greg Mortenson wrote a compelling memoir, *Three Cups of Tea*. It topped the *New York Times* bestseller list and remained a bestseller for over four years. It included stories about his harrowing journeys into Pakistan and his efforts to support the vulnerable in the country.

He founded an organization, Central Asia Institute (CAI), and raised tens of millions of dollars to fund the creation of schools for Pakistani girls. His heroism compelled President Obama to give $100,000 to CAI as one of ten nonprofits to whom he donated his Nobel Peace Prize winnings.[4]

Mortenson's story was compelling, but as investigations in 2011 uncovered, it was a fable, not a biography. Mortenson's accounts were fabricated. And his organization? Mostly a façade.

60 Minutes released the first of many exposés about Mortenson outlining his complex layers of lies. Author Jon Krakauer, a major donor and advocate for CAI, released his findings in a short book entitled *Three Cups of Deceit*. The book did not mince words:

> Mortenson has lied about the noble deeds he has done, the risks he has taken, the people he has met, the number of schools he has built. Moreover, Mortenson's charity . . . has issued fraudulent financial statements, and he has misused millions of dollars donated by school-children and other trusting devotees.[5]

The news of Mortenson's indiscretions surprised and angered his readers and donors. How could this happen? How could even the savviest of donors fall for the charade? How was this almost entirely made up?

Mortenson fleeced thousands of thoughtful people, including the most powerful man in the world. He raised over $70 million to fuel his pseudo-nonprofit. While Mortenson and CAI violated many nonprofit best practices,[6] the most blatant was the impotence and impropriety of the CAI board of directors.

At the time of the *60 Minutes* piece, only three people sat on the CAI board, one of whom was Mortenson. Two independent board members could not sufficiently monitor and govern an organization of this scope. In his critique, Krakauer stated:

> The entire board consisted of [Mortenson] and two submissive acolytes he could steamroll or ignore. With nobody left to hold him account-able, it appeared as though Greg had been stricken with a virulent strain of megalomania, leading him to believe he was exempt from the ethical codes that guide the behavior of ordinary mortals and other charities. He seemed to think he could lie about almost anything and get away with it.[7]

If the CAI board understood its mandate, they could have prevented, or at least uncovered, Mortenson's wrongdoings. Instead,
they failed to protect the mission of CAI, simply serving as high-five
friends for Mortenson as he masqueraded as a hero. It took investiga-
tive journalism, rather than basic nonprofit governance, to unearth
the grave malpractice.

"When a ministry encounters failure—or even worse, scandal—its
difficulties can almost always be traced to a breakdown in governance,"
states the Evangelical Council for Financial Accountability, the premier
accreditation agency dedicated to faith-based organizations. "The
importance of an active, informed governing body cannot be over-
emphasized. Left unchecked, even minor board neglect can eventually
intrude upon the accountability and effectiveness of the ministry."[8]

Today, CAI is embroiled in lawsuits, has lost most of its support,
and has lost public trust. This is an outcome a healthy board could
have prevented.

Pulling the Trigger

Board members create the tenor and protect the mission from the
many threats opposing it. But when boards are unwilling to fulfill
their roles, the mission will drift. Preventing collapses like the one
at Central Asia Institute starts and stops with the board members.

Terry Looper, board member for a number of large nonprofits,
believes the biggest weakness facing boards of faith-based organizations is their unwillingness to make hard decisions.

Even in cases where the leader is clearly taking an organization off
course, genuine accountability is rare. "I learned the hard lesson that
the paid CEO will win every time over the volunteer board member,"
Looper shared. "Unless you fire them."[9]

Among Christians, particularly, it is painful to fire staff, criticize
performance, and demand excellence. But the Bible isn't silent on this
issue. The narrative of Scripture paints a picture of God's character
with a beautiful balance of both grace and justice.

Proverbs, for example, says, "Whoever rebukes a man will afterward
find more favor than he who flatters with his tongue,"[10] and "Wounds
from a friend can be trusted, but an enemy multiplies kisses."[11]

Hard conversations are just that. They're hard. But board members must be willing to ask difficult questions and hold the executive leader accountable to the full mission of the organization. When boards do that, they put guardrails around the mission. They thwart drift before it starts.

"The best board members challenge assumptions and sharpen the focus of the organization," reflected Don Wolf, a seasoned business executive who serves on a number of boards. "A great board keeps the executive leadership team accountable and ultimately ensures the organization fulfills its potential."[12]

Easter and Christmas Churchgoers

I (Peter) serve on the boards of a number of great faith-based organizations. Near the conclusion of a recent conference call board meeting, the chair stated, "The final item of business is to vote on a new board member."

He continued, "John[13] is an industry leader. He was just voted one of the most influential people in America. He literally wrote the book about our industry. He has trained the best of the best. There truly is no one more capable than John and he will bring wisdom, financial support, and connections like we've never had before. I can't believe he wants to join our board!"

You could hear the excitement. Others added their amazement that John would want to join the board. Right before the vote, a fellow board member timidly chimed in, "This is amazing! John sounds like an all-star. But does anyone know about his faith?"

There was a moment of awkward silence until the board member who nominated him spoke up, "I'm not sure. We never really talked about that." No one else had either, even though faith was a vital part of the organization's mission.

Faith-based organizations don't often suffer from an inexhaustible supply of resources. We need to be opportunists. And it is tempting to add "heavy-hitters" to the board who are comfortable with our mission, even if they do not fully believe or practice core faith in their own lives.

He's supportive of our mission, we state. *She doesn't believe it all
personally, but she's totally fine that this is who we are*, we reason. *We
aren't looking for him to be a pastoral influence on the board; he's simply providing financial expertise we desperately need*, we plead. *Serving on our board might actually bring him closer to Christ*, we hope.

But if board members aren't bleeding for the mission, drift will
always trickle down. They must be the most passionate about the full
mission of the organization. If they aren't, conflict about the Christian
distinction of the organization will eventually surface.

When interviewing a candidate for the board, sometimes the cursory questions just don't provide the information boards need to
make informed decisions. Chris Crane, president and CEO of Edify,
a global faith-based organization, felt this on a recent board interview. He learned a very wealthy and influential board candidate was
a Christian and attended church.

The candidate could change the trajectory of the organization if
he joined the mission. But Crane knew he needed to press further.
Edify's work is overt in its Christian distinctiveness. "What does your
church involvement look like?" he asked.

"I go to church. Twice a year, on Christmas and Easter," the candidate shared. He was not invited onto the board.[14]

No Turning Back

The board I served on was in a bind. John's candidacy was tenuous.
Because he had already been asked to consider board membership,
it would have been a relational mess to change course. He had said
he would be willing to serve and was planning on joining the next
board meeting in person. He had too much influence in the industry
to risk offending him.

To prevent Mission Drift, organizations require as much process,
rigor, and intentionality in recruiting board members as they do in
recruiting key executives. Yet often the process lacks consistency or
even a clear method. If a high-powered person like John expresses
an interest in the mission, we sidestep the process and move forward
at full speed. Slack board recruitment is one of the primary causes
of Mission Drift.

Over the past few years, the board at Taylor University has recognized how important board nomination and selection truly is. They have thrown out generalizations and simple yes-and-no questions in favor of clear expectations about their board members.

"It starts at the top," said Mark Taylor, chair of the Taylor University board. And that's why Taylor's board recreated their nomination process and tightened their expectations.[15] Attending church twice a year wouldn't meet the threshold. For candidates to serve on the board at Taylor and other Mission True organizations, they must take their own faith as seriously as the organizations do.

"You must be very careful in selecting board members," shared Merv Auchtung, COO of Bethany Christian Services, the largest faith-based adoption ministry in the world. "They can keep us on the 'straight and narrow,' so to speak."[16]

Something as simple as having each potential board member write their faith story and sign an organizational statement of faith helps ensure that the guardians of the mission are in agreement with what they're charged with protecting.

Throughout this book, we try to be sensitive to the varied sectors, dynamics, and values of faith-based organizations. We avoid explicit "how-to" lists and black-and-white principles, instead sharing stories and case studies to provide leaders the right questions to ask.

But this principle is simply too important to skirt around. If the Christian distinctiveness of your organization is something you desire to protect, you cannot budge on the character and caliber of your board. If you go back to the stories of Harvard, Yale, ChildFund, the Y, the Pew Trusts, and the many others we found in our research, poor board selection and governance was always one of the driving causes of drift.

If the board isn't composed of folks who live out the values of the organization they lead, the organization will drift. The organization will secularize. It will only be a matter of time.

Tying Successors' Hands

"Anyone sincere about keeping to the mission must have safeguards in place or plan on Mission Drift," shared Chris Crane.[17] Over decades of for-profit and nonprofit board experience, he has seen how easy it is for organizations to lose sight of their founding purpose. So he creatively asked his board to bind the hands of future leaders of their organization to their core mission.

He was inspired by Wess Stafford's leadership at Compassion International. As president at Compassion, Stafford recognized how important his board was to guarding and fueling Compassion's mission.

"The quickest path to losing your spiritual way is through whom you put on your board," Stafford stated. "It's easy to get enamored with celebrity, with powerful names or deep pockets. One of the biggest mistakes nonprofits make, even Christian ones, is to confuse their board with their major donor program."[18]

So Stafford did something about it. He bound the hands of all future Compassion boards. Together with his board, they instituted a policy to cement their core mission. The policy, in summary, demanded a unanimous board vote—from all board members, not just those present at the meeting—in three consecutive years in order to unearth Compassion from its overtly Christian identity.

When Crane learned about Stafford and Compassion's insight on protecting their mission, he decided to propose a similar policy within his organization, Edify. And the policy was approved. The board resolution reads:

> We will seek to include Christian teaching and principles in every aspect of our work. It is hereby resolved that this primary purpose cannot be changed unless there are unanimous votes of 100% of all then duly elected members of the Edify Board of Directors at face-to-face meetings in three consecutive years.[19]

In other words, Edify won't allow itself to exist without Christ. Crane founded Edify and is unwilling to see his organization slip into secularization.

Mission True Boards

Mission True boards exhibit all the qualities of healthy boards. But they must also model an unwavering approach to safeguarding the mission of the organizations they govern. Mission True boards:

1. *Recruit carefully and prayerfully:* In appendix 1, we have included a simple board member nomination form to help you recruit engaged and humble leaders.

2. *Hold the chief executive responsible for the mission:* They are unafraid of making hard decisions and do not bend on areas core to the mission.

3. *Follow standard board practices:* The Evangelical Council for Financial Accountability outlines a number of simple practices to avoid the fate of organizations like the Central Asia Institute.[20]

4. *Create policies and safeguards:* Tie the hands of your successors by clarifying and specifying the importance of your organization's Christian distinctiveness. In appendix 2, we have included the board resolution created by Edify International.

5. *Remember the mission:* They keep the core values, history, and purpose of the organization central to their meetings and model these values in their own lives.

At the end of the book, we have included a number of resources for further reading on board governance and the other Mission True qualities we will cover. One chapter does not provide enough space to explore all the rich and important thinking on effective governance and organizational leadership. We hope to open up the right conversations on these topics, and these terrific resources will give you the tools you need to drill deeper.

Reading Aloud

As mentioned in an earlier chapter, the board members at The Crowell Trust—who are elected for lifetime terms—read aloud the charter written by Henry Crowell at their annual board meetings. Likewise, at Taylor, board members state aloud the mission of the university.

Board members at Crowell and Taylor know they need to bleed for the missions of the organizations they lead. Each must understand the mission, live the mission, and defend the mission. They need to have more than impressive academic credentials and balance sheets. They must embody the values of the organizations they lead.

Reading the charter and mission aloud grounds the board members in their purpose. They speak the words as an audible reminder to everyone around the table. As simple as this practice is, it reinforces the identity and increases the likelihood that decisions will be made according to their core purpose and identity.

When we were faced with the decision about whether or not to accept funding from the Houston oil and gas corporation that tied their funding to watering down our faith, our board provided guidance. They did not give us a quick answer. They wrestled with it. They wondered if we could find a "third way" forward where we accepted the donation, but didn't compromise on our mission. But in the end, they came to a unanimous decision: Based on our identity and core purpose, if those strings were attached to the gift, we needed to graciously decline the donation.

Our board understood their role as guardians. They prayerfully examined the options and spoke unanimously that our mission was not for sale. Remaining Mission True was their highest priority.

Great boards realize that they are the guardians of the mission, even though they are volunteers. They understand one of their key responsibilities is to recruit and support a leader whose full-time job is to protect the mission—and how easy it is for this one person to dramatically lead an organization off course.

8

TRUE LEADERSHIP

Mission True leaders set the cultural tone for the organization

A few years ago, Dr. J. Robert Clinton, Fuller Seminary professor, did a study that revealed alarming results. Analyzing biblical leaders, he found that only one out of three maintained a dynamic relationship with God and didn't abuse his or her power.

Only one in three finished well. And Clinton made the case that the ratio among Christian leaders is similar, if not worse, today.[1] Without focusing on the heart, leaders are at risk. This should sound the alarm for organizations desiring to remain Mission True. While important, a fantastic and engaged board, alone, is insufficient to protect against drift.

The author of Proverbs says, "Above all else, guard your heart, for it is the wellspring of life."[2] The heart is not only the wellspring of life; it's also the wellspring of organizational health. At the heart of an organization is its leader, and no faster way exists to get an organization off mission or tear down its credibility than through a fallen leader.

In *The Screwtape Letters,* C. S. Lewis gives us an inside glimpse of the war tactics of the enemy. In it, the demon Screwtape mentors his nephew, Wormwood, to disrupt the flourishing of the Kingdom. His tactic: attack the personal character and faith of the Christ-follower. And do so slowly: "Indeed the safest road to Hell is the gradual one—the gentle slope, soft underfoot, without sudden turnings, without milestones, without signposts."[3]

Undermining the personal integrity of leaders undercuts entire organizations. An organization's strength of mission is critically tied to the personal life of its leaders. To safeguard the mission, we must safeguard our hearts.

"It Couldn't Happen to Me"

Carrying out a study of ministry leaders, Dr. Howard Hendricks of Dallas Theological Seminary interviewed 246 individuals who had committed sexual immorality within a two-year period. Hendricks sought to determine key factors that led to their fall.

Of these 246 individuals, all believed they were incapable of committing their moral failing.

If you believe you are immune, then you are most vulnerable.

Additionally, all had fallen away from spending daily time with the Lord in prayer. None had an accountability partner.[4]

Even if a leader doesn't fall publicly, a leader whose heart is not rooted in Christ and actively growing can be just as devastating to a ministry. Jesus said, "Apart from me you can do nothing."[5] Jesus didn't say we can do *little* separate from Him. He said *nothing.*

A leader not deeply grounded in prayer and spiritual disciplines is a leader susceptible to Mission Drift.

A few years ago, our organization experienced rapid growth. Due to an incredible group of dedicated staff members, donors, and key partnerships, we extended our network from 5,000 entrepreneurs to over 500,000 in eight years. Fundraising revenue grew tenfold. We celebrated our millionth loan. I (Peter) wrote a book on microfinance with a friend, had speaking engagements, and traveled extensively.

But while ministry was thriving, internally I was at my lowest. I was traveling over a hundred nights a year. My family was not flourishing. Growth and advancing our mission became so important to me that I was giving my family my leftovers.

So focused on what I was doing, I forgot who I was becoming. My prayer and spiritual life had been marginalized in the pursuit of growing "my" ministry.

We grew faster than our capacity to implement with excellence. I became so proud of our growth that the quality and Christ-centeredness of our mission took a back seat. Too busy implementing programs, I gave inadequate attention to personal growth and deeper discipleship.

An attitude of "I'll spend time with Christ when my inbox is empty" meant I was spending very little time listening in prayer or learning from the Word.

Incremental, slow, *personal* mission creep often leads to organizational mission creep. Mission True leaders not growing in Christ lead their organizations with feet on shaky ground.

Yes, they may get a lot done, but without a healthy dependence on God, it is futile striving. Psalms says, "Unless the Lord builds the house, the builders labor in vain."[6]

Humbition

"The greatest idol I find in leaders is ambition," said Brennan Manning, author of *The Ragamuffin Gospel,* to a group of megachurch pastors.[7]

The allure of success and growth can lead to some pretty dangerous situations for both the leader of an organization and the organization itself.

Fred Smith, president of The Gathering, a community of Christian givers, said that his main concern for leaders today is our modern emphasis on branding and image. "Our platforms become the gallows upon which our humility is hanged," Smith said.[8] Obsessed with appearance and our reputation, it is easy to fall into the trap of pride.

And pride can have devastating effects on a company or organization. In *How the Mighty Fall,* business writer Jim Collins says the first step toward a company's destruction is "hubris born of success."[9] It's an attitude, not an external factor. Pride leads us to adopt the wrong definition of success. When we begin to see our priority as a growing ministry, instead of a faithful one, we sow the seeds of drift.

As Collins noted, self-centeredness may lead to short-term success, but it often undermines an organization long-term.

One of our friends and heroes is Ruth Callanta. Though Callanta is only five feet tall, she is a giant of faith and models tenacious "hum-bition" (humility + ambition).[10] Callanta leads the Center for Community Transformation (CCT), an organization lifting up the name of Jesus and serving the Philippines' financially poor.

When she was young, she recognized her life's purpose: to address poverty in the Philippines. She has an impressive résumé. Before her work at CCT, she was well known throughout the world as a leading expert on development. She worked for the World Bank. She led Philippine Business for Social Progress, an organization facilitating poverty alleviation efforts between business and nonprofits.

But throughout her travels and work, she began to see a common theme: The aid and development community was inhibited because of pride and ambition. International agencies came in and truly believed they had all the solutions—so they steamrolled over the local citizens and imposed ill-fitting solutions.

She set out to change that dynamic. In order to educate the next generation in right practices of development, she attended the prestigious Asian Institute of Management, based in Manila, and connected with Harvard Business School.

Yet she came to the conclusion that even the very best development programs weren't enough. Greed, pride, and self-centeredness keep even the noblest intentions from effectively working.

> In the Philippines, we had implemented practically every development intervention that had ever been formulated, adapted, and recycled. Immense resources were being poured into development projects.
>
> Why are the poor still poor? Why are communities still unchanged? I became convinced that unless people's hearts were changed, there could not be any true transformation. We are too self-centered, too selfish to be able to make a difference in the lives of other people.

Of course, when I realized that, I also realized that there was only One who could change the hearts of people: the Lord Jesus Christ![11]

Callanta has led a vibrant organization for decades, but even more impressive is how she has kept her hands and heart focused on faithful servant leadership. She still rises early for "dawn watch" prayer as she gathers to watch the sun rise and pray with a team of leaders.[12] While visiting the Philippines, we woke at 4 a.m. to join Callanta. Kneeling on small bamboo mats with Callanta and her team, I found the position uncomfortable and the hour unappealing, but I will never forget her earnest prayers or heartfelt praise for a brand-new day to serve.

Callanta knows the core of faithful leadership is a daily focus on Christ.

Why Wilberforce Persevered

When we forget to feed our faith and cement our foundation, we become vulnerable to burnout and overextension, which will inevitably harm the mission. We need to build our lives on a firm foundation.

Reformers who have "gone the distance" and finished strong understand the connection between inner spiritual growth and faithful service. Consider one of the most celebrated social activists of the nineteenth century, William Wilberforce.

Most people know him as the man who spent his life committed to abolishing slavery, overcoming seemingly impossible challenges as he did so. For thirty years, up until he died, he fought the fight against slavery. And he credits his faith and his roots for upholding him.

His challenges were great: Not only was he threatening the very foundation of the British Empire through campaigning for a cause that would disrupt Britain's financial power and global position, but he also went practically blind, suffered from ulcerated bowels, became addicted to doctor-prescribed opium, and his spine was so curved he needed a brace to keep his head from resting on his chest.

Wilberforce was a man with a cause. But much more important, he was a man with a foundation. He stated, "You can't endure in bearing fruit if you sever the root."[13] The root for him was a firmly held belief in God's atoning work on the cross and a lifetime of spiritual disciplines.

Wilberforce reminds us to remember the central place of God-centered, Christ-exalting faith.

Mission True organizations are obsessed with issues of the heart. They believe everything we do is downstream from who we are. Without attention to our personal faith, we are without an anchor and left to drift.

Through words, actions, and behaviors, leaders either undermine or reinforce the mission.

Predictable Faithfulness

Recently, an acquaintance of mine told me a story from a time early in his career when he was working as a sales representative for a financial services company. As he made a courtesy call, he was severely berated by their largest customer.

Following the encounter, he reported the treatment to his supervisor.

Though the confrontation occurred with the company's most influential customer, the supervisor responded, "If that's the way they treat you, then that's not a customer we want to keep."

And his supervisor picked up the phone, called the customer, and said the company was no longer interested in their business.

The supervisor's response showed the character and values of the company. Clearly, this company valued its people over short-term profits.

As I heard this story, the point that made an indelible impression with me was that this incident showed the underlying culture, a culture that was highly predictable: Leaders always acted in accordance with their beliefs, even when it caused financial loss or hardship. The result was unparalleled levels of trust and employee engagement.

Often in much less dramatic ways, Mission True leaders constantly make decisions to strengthen, rather than diminish, the mission. It's not just what we do. It's not who we say we are. It's how we act.

In matters of integrity and service, Mission True leaders are highly predictable. They act in accordance with the organization's beliefs every single time. Employees do not waste energy wondering if leaders will do the right thing.

Mission True organizations are fanatical about modeling and developing leaders who fully embody the mission.

Focused Faithfulness

By all accounts, Billy Graham has lived a life consistent with the message he shared. After being in the spotlight for over six decades, you would think squalors of controversy would surround him, and yet his organization and reputation are untainted. How did he live faithfully?

In a desire to learn from his example, we read *The Leadership Secrets of Billy Graham* by Harold Myra and Marshall Shelley. Turns out, Graham understood the connection between his personal life and his ministry.

Early in his ministry, he identified that "spiritual enthusiasm [does] not make you immune to greed, pride, lust, and ambition."[14]

In 1948, as a leader of Youth For Christ, he created safeguards to protect his heart and his team's reputation. Meeting in Modesto, California, the team individually brainstormed every temptation they could imagine encountering. When they met corporately, they discovered "the lists were remarkably similar"[15] and included:

1. *Shady handling of money.* The temptation here was to "wring as much money as possible out of an audience, often with strong emotional appeals."[16] Graham and his team understood the seductiveness of greed and the possibility of taking advantage of the audiences who came to hear their presentations. As a result, they intentionally downplayed the offering and created a fundraising plan dependent on funds raised by local committees to avoid the allegation of financial impropriety.

2. *Sexual Immorality.* The team identified that one of the most difficult strains on traveling evangelists was the time spent away from their families, which opened up doors to inappropriate behavior. In Graham's words, "We pledged among ourselves to avoid any situation that would have even the appearance of compromise or suspicion."[17] Citing as a core verse 2 Timothy 2:22: "Flee . . . youthful lusts" (KJV), they committed to not being

alone with women other than their wives. When they had a
meeting with someone of the opposite sex, they did it in "an
uncompromising way." Essentially, this meant meeting in public.

3. *Exaggerated accomplishments.* A "minor" moral lapse of not
telling the truth was (and is) a temptation for people on stage.
But this small compromise becomes the gateway to larger moral
issues. Graham knew there were no "small sins" and decided to
put procedures in place to promote truth-telling. For example,
instead of exaggerating the size of an audience, Graham and his
team accepted crowd size estimates from the police and other
officials, even if they believed there were more people in atten-
dance. Also, rather than calling people who came forward at
events "converts," they chose to identify people as "inquirers."

These principles became portions of the "Modesto Manifesto."[18]
Soon after Graham skyrocketed to fame, yet he remained grounded.[19]
Graham understood how his actions could impact his ministry and
was unswerving in his commitment to integrity.

Mission True Leaders

Graham took the "Modesto Manifesto" one step further. He gathered
together influential individuals to create a board of accountability,
those with authority to supervise the decisions of the evangelism
team.[20] Even Graham submitted to the board, not trying to tiptoe
around them or find loopholes for his own benefit.

He believed he needed people who could tell him the truth at all
times, even when it was uncomfortable. Mission True leaders:

1. *Admit vulnerability:* They never forget their own sinfulness.
Because of the magnitude of their mission, they know the stakes
are too high to place faith in their own strength.

2. *Invite others in:* They invite close friends and family to speak
honestly and candidly into their lives. They welcome and cher-
ish challenges and accountability from their circle of trusted
friends.

3. *Create safeguards against impropriety:* They build guardrails like Billy Graham did to help ward off moral failure.

4. *Remain in the vine:* They know their fruitfulness and success depends entirely on the One who sustains. They prioritize their faith and practice spiritual disciplines with regularity.[21]

Said plainly, Mission True leaders remain in Jesus. We celebrate the lives of William Wilberforce, Ruth Callanta, and Billy Graham. They have modeled the connection between their own integrity and the impact of the organizations they lead.

> Abide in me, and I in you. As the branch cannot bear fruit by itself, unless it abides in the vine, neither can you, unless you abide in me. I am the vine; you are the branches. Whoever abides in me and I in him, he it is that bears much fruit, for apart from me you can do nothing.[22]

C12, a leadership organization, understands the need to cultivate Mission True leaders and created an annual survey instrument to help their members explore whether they are growing in the essential attributes of Mission True Leadership. To assess your leadership, consider taking their survey included on our web site (www.mission driftbook.com).

Mission True leaders abide in Christ. But they don't just practice this personally. They also know they are incapable of leading on their own. They are relentless in their pursuit of fellow Mission True leaders who model these qualities at all levels of the organization.

9

IMPRESSIVE CREDENTIALS ARE NOT ENOUGH

Mission True organizations hire first and foremost for heart and character

On the outside, Big Idea was the poster child for Christian ministry.

The maker of *Veggie Tales* was likened to a Christian Disney, and its computer-animated characters Larry the Cucumber and Bob the Tomato brought Christian values to the living rooms of families across the country. At its peak, Big Idea—based in Chicago—was the largest animation studio between the coasts, employing over 200 people with revenues in excess of $40 million.[1]

Though a booming company, internally Big Idea had an identity problem. Their executive team struggled to clarify who they were and where they were going.

Aided by an external consultant, the management team spent a day trying to get everyone on board with the core mission. But no one agreed.

Finally, Phil Vischer, Big Idea's founder, stood up to share his founding vision.

"I am a Christian," I said, "and I believe the Bible exclusively holds the truth about our standing before God and the path to restore our relationships with him. I want to share that truth with our culture. That is, at the end of the day, what Big Idea is about."

Vischer didn't receive the response he expected.

His president of two years said, "If that's what this is about, I need to opt out."

In his personal account of Big Idea's demise, Vischer writes:

> The room went deathly silent. I felt like a complete idiot. The man I had hired to help me accomplish my mission lacked my motivation entirely. I was mortified to realize that my failure to get to know him before—or after—offering him the most important job in the company had greatly contributed to the organizational mess my ministry had become.[2]

Soon after, Big Idea went bankrupt. Internal strife hurt their sales. They just didn't have a leadership team all rowing in the same direction.

The Mission Drift Generation

The founder has a clear calling and vision. No one is more passionate about the cause.

"The mission keeps founders awake at night, and it drives them during the day," said Marty Caldwell, senior vice president at Young Life.[3]

But the founder's passion rarely translates to subsequent generations of leadership. Too often, the passions of the first generation become the preferences of the second generation and are irrelevant to the third generation.[4]

Scripture contains numerous examples of this reality. Consider the second chapter of Judges. The story starts with an affirmation of Joshua's leadership: "The people served the Lord throughout the lifetime of Joshua and of the elders who outlived him and who had seen all the great things the Lord had done for Israel."[5]

But after Joshua's successful leadership, the nation forgot its foundation.

After that whole generation had been gathered to their ancestors, another generation grew up who knew neither the Lord nor what he had done for Israel. Then the Israelites did evil in the eyes of the Lord and served the Baals. They forsook the Lord, the God of their ancestors, who had brought them out of Egypt.[6]

Just one generation before, the Israelites took possession of the Promised Land. Finally, they received their destiny. But how quickly they turned their backs on God.

Within only one generation after incredible miracles, the people of Israel were functional atheists. They forgot the God who led them into the Promised Land. They forgot the miracles of the walls of Jericho. They forgot they were a chosen people. And they turned to Baal and set up Ashtoreth poles.[7]

Their spiritual amnesia had devastating consequences—whenever they went to battle, the "hand of the Lord was against them to defeat them."[8]

This is also true of the House of David. King David was a man after God's own heart.[9] His son Solomon followed God sporadically, swayed by his many foreign wives. And Solomon's son Rehoboam completely disregarded the God of his grandfather David. Because of Rehoboam's leadership, "Judah did evil in the eyes of the Lord. By the sins they committed they stirred up his jealous anger more than those who were before them had done."[10]

In the examples, the second or third generation has blatantly disregarded the faith of their grandparents. The current of drift in hiring is strong. Without careful and prayerful hiring practices, by the third generation, "you may be *unrecoverably* lost from your original vision and mission," said Caldwell.

The Whole Enchilada

Excellent organizations know the importance of hiring. They refuse to settle.

For example, consulting giant McKinsey often interviews individuals eight times prior to selecting a team member. McKinsey also chooses only 1 percent of the 200,000 applicants they annually interview.[11]

Leading organizations are patient in hiring and believe an open position, no matter how painful, is still better than a position filled with the wrong person.

What is true in the private sector is intensified for Christ-centered organizations placing a premium on finding people who are serious and intentional about their faith. Practically, this means the recruitment process requires the search committee to look beyond sparkling résumés. As much attention as technical competency receives, screening for culture and mission should receive even more.

Mission True organizations we interviewed tended to have a "hire slow and fire fast"[12] mentality and grasped the consequences of having the wrong person representing the mission. They also seemed to have a diverse selection committee and always included "mission fit" as a key part of the interview process.

"Close enough" just isn't "good enough" for Mission True organizations, said Phil Smith, who has served as CEO and chairman of several publicly traded companies. "It is not your enemies you have to worry about, it is your supporters and employees who 'almost' have the vision. Eat the whole enchilada, or go somewhere else."[13]

Mission True employees are hungry for the whole enchilada.

DNA

Driving in a van across potholed roads in rural Dominican Republic, we finally arrived at our destination: not the beautiful beaches or resorts, but a modest wooden home with roosters providing the background music. As we exited the van, the sound of laughter greeted our group. We were visiting a Young Life club.

Although I could not understand the Spanish, I (Peter) knew exactly what was happening in front of us. The opening songs created a relaxed environment. The hilarious and slightly ridiculous games broke down barriers. The talk brought the truth of the Gospel to these students in a way they could understand.

The context was different, but what I was watching had exactly the same DNA as the Young Life meetings I've been to in Texas, Pennsylvania, and Massachusetts.

The centerpiece of the entire model was the Young Life staff. Young Life hires and then trains their staff with their mission in mind. They know what they are about. Their staffing decisions create mission clarity. Whether in the Dominican Republic or Dallas, Young Life models Mission True hiring.

Conversely, when there is cloudiness about mission, hiring at faith-based organizations quickly becomes problematic.

"Golden Rule Christians"

Conference breakout sessions typically make me (Chris) want to break out my smartphone or break out of the room. But at a recent conference for human resources professionals, one breakout session was full of fireworks about a controversial subject—hiring at faith-based organizations. What the speaker shared, however, left me disheartened.

The presenter—let's call her Sharon—hailed from one of the largest faith-based organizations in the world. Her organization is consistently platformed at major evangelical churches and conferences across the country as an organization fulfilling Christ's call to bring hope to the least and the lost. Sharon directed their global hiring efforts across dozens of countries. As a member of the executive team and as "final say" on all senior leadership positions, her stamp carried significant credence. Sharon led a breakout session on recruitment and hiring, her domains of expertise.

She flipped through PowerPoint slides with ease, articulating how she screened job candidates and recruited for positions in remote countries. Sharon concluded her talk, and the audience thanked her with a round of gentle applause. And that's when things got interesting.

The conference included folks of a wide swath of religious beliefs—apathetics, atheists, humanists, evangelicals, Muslims, and everyone in between. One questioner, based on his tone, was likely a practicing antagonist, if you can call that a religion. I remember their exchange vividly.

Antagonist: You say you're a Christian faith-based organization. Does that mean you only hire Christians?

Sharon: Well, we hire Christians for our senior leadership positions in the countries where we work, but let me state with absolute clarity: We have a strict non-evangelism policy and hire people of all faiths for entry- and mid-level positions. We're about helping people, not about telling them what they should believe.

Antagonist: So you do discriminate in your leadership roles. Well, how do you know if someone is a Christian?

Sharon: We don't discriminate. When I say "Christian," I mean we aim to hire leaders exhibiting the Golden Rule—those who love their neighbors like themselves. Good people exhibiting kindness and humility. We look for those traits in interviewees.

Antagonist: OK, so say you do hire a Muslim or Hindu for a mid-level position: Could that person be promoted to a senior leadership role?

Sharon: Absolutely. We have numerous Muslims and Hindus, in fact, serving as country directors for us across the globe.

The conversation continued for some time, the antagonist and Sharon each feeling each other out, like boxers at the weigh-in ceremony. After their brief exchange, I replayed Sharon's responses over and over again, attempting to reconcile what she said with what I read on her organization's web site.

I walked away from the breakout session confused. How could her organization deploy this sort of hiring approach and still hope to accomplish its full mission?

What I expected would be a blah breakout session became a personal watershed moment. The gravitational pull of secularism is felt perhaps most acutely in hiring.

The approach advocated by Sharon fails the sniff test. It's inconsistent with Scripture and dangerous ground legally. It might receive more public acceptance and less media criticism, but it will lead to drift as those staffing decisions compound and multiply over time. When another faith-based organization decided to stand strong on their hiring process, national news outlets showed up. And they weren't there to cheer them on.

Help Wanted

World Relief experienced a wake-up call when they decided to implement a statement of faith for all of their employees. The move was generally well received—except in one office. Though they had always been an implicitly Christian organization, the staff in one of World Relief's key offices in the United States reacted strongly against the decision.

Almost three quarters of their staff in that office resigned in protest or were terminated.[14]

It wasn't an easy transition. They were heavily criticized by news publications. Legally, organizations with a centrally religious purpose and identity are allowed to hire on the basis of faith.[15] Still, the event fueled energetic discussions about their core identity and the role of faith in relief and development organizations.

In a *Chicago Tribune* article on the issue, an employee, then director of immigrant legal services, said of World Relief's decision, "It's legal, but it's ridiculously wrong and un-Christian." She left her post with World Relief shortly thereafter.

The article, titled "Help Wanted, but Only Christians Need Apply," highlighted the challenges faith-based organizations face in their hiring policies. But World Relief responded to the criticism with conviction.

"We felt we needed to put a formal policy in place that reflects a 65-year history of hiring according to our faith," Stephan Bauman, president and CEO, said. "The policy is really just to galvanize our organization."[16]

The staff departures from the World Relief Chicago office were ultimately not a result of a policy. They were the result of a clear identity. World Relief is not simply a social agency. If they were that alone, the employee might be right in her critique. But World Relief's mission extends beyond the material help of immigrants and refugees. This is where Bauman was right. And his decision did galvanize.

Purposeful Hiring

Black-and-white rules are always clearest. For two summers during high school, I (Chris) worked as a ride operator at Dutch Wonderland family amusement park. I donned the coolest of elastic shorts and loud emblem-adorned polo shirts. In the park, I drove the monorail, monitored the log flume, and worked the Sky Princess, our retro wooden roller coaster. But on every ride, we had one clear rule: Height is nonnegotiable.

Yes, I wielded the height-stick. This fear-inducing measuring stick held the line on who could ride and who could not. I was the teenager who made countless children cry. And at times, I received the condescending scorn of parents who felt their children were "much more mature than their heights." *Nope*, I would say. *Nice try with the height-adding hair gel, lady, but he's got a few months till he's ready to conquer the Sky Princess* (as an aside to parents: no savvy ride operator is fooled by the hair gel sham).

The rule was clear. Our insurance policies depended on it. And our supervisors were (rightly) insistent that we hold a firm line on height. But it's not this clear for faith-based organizations. The more we researched, the more we realized how important—and yet how challenging—hiring practices can be.

For example, a policy of hiring Christians only could actually impede the work of Mission True organizations. HOPE works in one country where it is illegal to hire only Christians. We have seen many Christian organizations evicted from the country because of their disregard for this law.

In this place, our mission has a different flavor than in a country like Rwanda or Ukraine, but our Christian distinctiveness and mission go on there with the same vibrancy, focused primarily on our leaders discipling and teaching staff members through intentional long-term relationships.

In our research, we learned about a unique hiring approach deployed by Joshua Station in Denver. This housing ministry helps families transition from homelessness to permanent housing and stability. They thoughtfully address the whole-person needs of the families they serve. Their Christian caseworkers mentor, encourage, and cheer on Joshua Station families along their journey.

But they don't hire Christians exclusively. They often hire front desk workers for their ministry who have successfully graduated from Joshua Station. These workers are not always Christians. But these employees understand and believe in the mission of Joshua Station. And they are invited to participate in staff devotions, prayer times, and other activities unique to a faith-based housing program.

"We've hired a handful of Joshua Station graduates who weren't followers of Jesus," shared Jeff Johnsen, founder and executive director. "A couple of those have made commitments to Christ. The others have opened up to the life of the Christian community. I feel good that they'll meet Jesus when the time is right."[17]

What differentiates World Relief and Joshua Station from Sharon's organization is that they hire with clarity and purpose. They employ Christians who can embody their mission. But they also intentionally employ those who are not Christians. When making hiring decisions, there are two questions we suggest faith-based organizations ask about their approach:

Is it prayerful?

Is it intentional?

If yes, then there is room for a number of thoughtful approaches. As much as a straightforward rule would make things simpler, the complexity of hiring demands a more nuanced approach.

Supreme Court Validation

Hiring is a touchy issue. With religious discrimination cases on the rise toward employers who screen by faith, we need to assert our case with clarity and confidence.

Dr. Stanley Carlson-Thies, perhaps the nation's foremost expert on faith-based organizations, founded the Institutional Religious Freedom Alliance and previously served in the White House Office of Faith-Based and Community Initiatives. He notes:

The U.S. has a strong tradition of religious freedom, but we may have become complacent about freedom for parachurch organizations. The landscape itself is starting to change. . . . Faith-based organizations and their leaders [need to] better understand and use their religious freedoms, and persuasively communicate why that freedom is important for society.[18]

We need to be capable of persuasively communicating the unique contributions our organizations make to the world—because of our Christian identity. And we need to develop language to explain why preferentially hiring Christians is necessary to do that.

In 2010, three World Vision employees were let go because they were unwilling to affirm the core tenets of Christian faith. World Vision took a lot of heat for their decision. And the case became public news when it was heard by the United States Supreme Court. Ultimately, the court validated World Vision's position.

Dean Owen, a spokesperson for World Vision, said hiring folks who affirm World Vision's faith convictions is nonnegotiable. "We do it because our faith is integral to our work," he said. "That's true whether it's our people overseeing relief programs in more than a hundred countries, or whether it's my friend Chuck, who runs our mailroom."[19]

World Vision took a tough position in firing three longstanding staff members. But the decision wasn't made on a whim. It was purposeful and aligned with their hiring approach. Clarity and consistency always win, especially when it comes to hiring.

Beware the Tipping Point

In our research, interviewees consistently discussed the principle of hiring well. Mission True leaders hire carefully, intentionally, and prayerfully. They approach each hiring decision seriously, recognizing that each staff member represents the mission of the organization.

"One of the primary reasons for Mission Drift is that people join your organization who are very excited about portions of your vision, but are either opposed to or don't care about the rest of it," noted Phil Smith.[20]

The drift at Big Idea (*Veggie Tales*), Harvard, and ChildFund was connected to their people. As shared earlier, Derek Bok, president at Harvard from 1971–1991, wrote a letter to Harvard's board and key supporters about the university's departure from its roots. Among other reasons, he described the hiring philosophy change.

"The practice of looking at the personal character of candidates for faculty appointment fell into disuse," Bok wrote. "Intellect and technical proficiency had decisively triumphed as the preeminent goals of the professoriat."[21]

Harvard's leaders cared more about credentials than Christian character. These staff members liked Harvard's intellectual rigor but didn't buy into the full mission. They "almost" had the vision. And those hiring decisions, compounded over time, led Harvard to a place where they could no longer turn back to the values of their founding.

Chick-Fil-A models hiring excellence. Their people consistently carry the mission and values of the company forward in the way they do business and conduct themselves with customers. Their hiring strategy? It's quite simple.

> "First, we look for character," shared Dee Ann Turner, vice president of talent at Chick-Fil-A. "We are looking for someone who has a track record of good strong moral and ethical behavior and people who value serving others with a bias toward growing themselves and others. Second, we look for competency. . . . Third, we look for chemistry, the ability to fit in with our team."[22]

Using this simple hiring phrase, Chick-Fil-A has become one of the largest restaurant chains in the world, with perhaps the most distinctive and celebrated corporate culture. Because of Chick-Fil-A's leadership in this area, we have adopted their three C's in our hiring process: character, competence, and chemistry.

Mission True Hiring

When your founding values and core identity are no longer found in your current staff, you have a serious people problem. Either you've hired poorly or you have underestimated the importance of ongoing training and culture. Mission True leaders:

1. *Hire slow and fire fast:* Even if it causes pain in the organization, they wait for the right people who can carry the mission forward. If you have a staff member undermining the values and mission of your organization, the problem will not go away on its own. Act quickly.

2. *Clearly define your approach to hiring based on faith:* Be prayerful and intentional in hiring staff, recognizing staff cannot share what they do not have.

3. *Be consistent with your hiring policy:* The quickest way to a hiring discrimination lawsuit is using incoherent or inconsistent hiring standards.

4. *Inculcate staff in your values and history:* Hiring is just the beginning. Take the intentionality with which you screen candidates and embed it in your orientation and training practices.

Mission True leaders understand that the offer letter is only the first step. They quickly infect staff with the DNA of the organization. Young Life places a high value on hiring right. But their job offers are only the start of the hiring process. One of the practices they have used is a consistent oral story telling of the history and values of the organization.

"Storytelling is honored and sacred for Young Life," shared Marty Caldwell, vice president at Young Life.

Bob Mitchell, 80, is one of the key historians at Young Life. Having been one of the first young people changed by its programs, he later became its third president. [23] Though he no longer officially serves, every year he and his wife, Claudia, sit down with new Young Life staff. The Mitchells tell the stories of Young Life's beginnings.

"We are like the Hebrew nation," said Caldwell. "We are a story-telling clan. We are guarded by a written and oral history."[24]

This is Mission True hiring.

The pressures toward drift aren't just an internal problem, however. There are others with substantial influence, and often they are holding the organization's proverbial purse strings.

10

Follow the Money

Mission True organizations partner with
donors who believe in their full mission

Few people have changed higher education more than Andrew Carnegie. He understood the power of education and was intensely focused
in his pursuit of knowledge. As a child, for example, he walked five
miles each way to attend classes on bookkeeping. He took this intensity
to his business and success followed him.

After selling Carnegie Steel Company, one of his first actions was
to give $5 million to the New York Public Library. Later, he helped
found what is now Carnegie Mellon University.[1]

Propelled by his belief that teaching was among the most valuable
but underpaid professions, he made an extraordinary gift to provide
pensions for teachers in America. On April 28, 1905, the *New York
Times* headline regarding his contribution read:

In Carnegie's Letter of Gift, he made it clear that any religious
schools requiring students to adhere to a statement of belief or under
a religious governance structure would be excluded from his foundation's grants.[2]

110

CARNEGIE MILLIONS FOR COLLEGE PENSION FUND

$10,000,000 for Aged University and Technical School Teachers.

INCOME WILL BE $500,000

No Condition of Race, Sex, Creed, or Color, but Sectarian and State Institutions Are Barred.

Especially for schools facing financial challenges, the economic incentive caused administrators to put a dollar value on their church relationships and historical Christian identity. Often, money won.

You can imagine what those school administrator conversations might have been like. *Imagine the good it could do for our teachers and their families. We still know why we teach. Our policies and people won't change. Also, we're broke.*

Brown University, the first college founded by the Baptists[3], led the way in severing ties with its Baptist affiliation to receive funding. Other elite colleges like Dartmouth soon followed.[4]

One university to sever denominational ties and receive funding was Oberlin College—where Charles Finney, the renowned evangelist of the Second Great Awakening, resided as the college's president several decades earlier.

Carnegie's funding advanced secularism at an alarming pace throughout the country. Author of *Andrew Carnegie*, David Nasaw, writes, "It is doubtful that he had any idea, in doing so, of the unintended consequences of his action. . . . Carnegie pensions would, in a relatively short time, change the face of higher education in America."[5]

Financial incentives are a potent factor in Mission Drift, and it is not just a historical issue.

How Can You Say No?

Recently I (Peter) met Nico van der Merwe at a conference in Chicago. He described a recent situation that echoed the situation school administrators faced when they heard about Carnegie's funding a hundred years before.

Nico is a South African entrepreneur who made his fortune specializing in the circulation and delivery of Swiss hearing aids and audiological equipment and production of custom-made hearing protection devices for those working in mining.

God blessed Nico in business, and Nico chose to bless others by starting a school in South Africa that includes deaf children in mainstream classrooms where they learn alongside their hearing friends— without sign language. In 2002, his family built Eduplex Preschool, which provided 175 children with the highest quality education. As the children graduated from preschool, he felt God leading him to build a primary school.

Given his passion for the cause of the deaf, van der Merwe shared his idea persuasively with potential donors. It wasn't long before he attracted other key partners. His vision had traction with a growing portion of wealthy Swiss businesspeople.

The first phase of construction was completed, and school was in session. A local church also used the property for adult Bible study on Sundays. Since the school was empty, it just made sense to allow the church to hold meetings there on weekends.

But when the Swiss funders who promised to finance the primary school discovered the church, they delivered an unexpected mandate: Evict the church from the property or we will abandon our funding.[6]

Hearing Nico's story brought me right back to the boardroom overlooking Houston's skyline and to the power and influence of money. Especially when you're cash strapped and the offer is generous, how can you possibly say no?

Worse Than Terrorism?

Anyone who has ever worked for a nonprofit knows how much power donors hold. And it can often put Mission True organizations in a defensive position when they meet funders who are uncomfortable with their Christian distinctiveness.

During a meeting with a philanthropist at an event in Chicago, I had a brief but lively conversation with her about women's empowerment and the developing world. She encouraged me to apply to her foundation for funding.

However, on the foundation's web site, I read clear guidelines about the organizations they will not support. The second guideline prohibited organizations engaged in terrorist activities. The first guideline prohibited religious affiliation.

The threat of "terrorist activities or violence of any kind" took a back seat to the threat of the Gospel. Our culture is growing in its suspicion of anything faith-based—enough to rank "exposure" to the Good News as more dangerous than terrorism.

The Silent Majority

Philanthropy makes headlines when Bill Gates, Warren Buffett, and the major foundations announce their giving in press releases. Government funding can also be a significant source of income. Big checks create the illusion that the government and secular funders are giving the most financially, but the data tells a different story.

According to Giving USA, based on data collected each year from The Center on Philanthropy at Indiana University, U.S. charitable giving totaled $298.42 billion in 2011.[7] Of that, individuals (and bequests) gave 81 percent, while foundations and corporations combined gave 19 percent.[8]

Yet as we read and heard stories of Mission Drift, we were surprised how often corporate, government, and foundation donors drove the drift. Organizations compromised on their core values to woo these institutional funders, while ignoring individuals, who collectively give over four times as much. The sum of the many individuals is far greater than the sum of the few major foundations and corporate donors.

This myth drives boards of many faith-based organizations to water down their Christian distinctiveness. But our findings paint a much different picture. Feed My Starving Children (FMSC), a faith-based global food relief agency, is a case study for this.

Explosive Growth

Feed My Starving Children's (FMSC) charitable revenue had remained flat for ten years. Waffling in their Christian identity at the time, they began soft-pedaling their Christian faith to attract new donors.

"We put a nice secular face on the organization," shared Mark Crea, executive director of FMSC.

But the approach didn't rescue the organization. In 2003, operating on an annual budget of $830,000, the board and a handful of staff recognized they were heading in the wrong direction.

"We said, 'The work is good. The model works. There's a need for our service. But we don't have God,'" shared Crea.

They decided to hold a public ceremony rededicating FMSC to its roots in Christ. And everything changed from that point forward. In 2012, just nine years later, FMSC had annual revenue exceeding $35 million.

"What changed?" Crea asked. "Why did our revenue multiply over 42 times in nine years? Well, the only thing that changed was we rededicated our organization to Christ. For those of us leading, we are going to stop apologizing for our faith and stick to who we are." [9]

FMSC has received support not *in spite of* its convictions but *because* of them.

It's just one example of many organizations that have not been penalized by their mission commitment. Rather, the opposite appears to be true. Examining fundraising data from four Mission True organizations we profiled in this book, we discovered that all saw dramatic increases in both total revenue and numbers of donors over the past ten years. During that time charitable revenue of these organizations grew between 53 and 895 percent. The numbers of donors giving to these organizations grew between 12 and 1165 percent.

This isn't formulaic. Remaining Mission True certainly doesn't guarantee explosive growth in fundraising numbers. It does illustrate through real-life, concrete examples, however, that while conviction about your Christian commitment may drive some corporate and government funders away, Christian donors will rally when you are clear and bold about your faith.[10]

Money Talks

Mission True organizations recruit and engage Mission True donors. For the remainder of this chapter, we'd like to shift our attention from the organization to the donor. As donors, you have a critical role to play in helping the organizations you love stay the course.

It is easy to assume that these principles of generosity are only applicable to the wealthiest of philanthropists, but even grassroots givers need to be setting priorities and practices in place now to avoid unintended outcomes in the future.

"Follow the money" is what my friend Terry Looper says. Terry would know. He serves on several different boards, and he's seen firsthand the influence of funding.

Donors are an accurate predictor of whether or not an organization is going to deviate off mission. Specifically, what excites and motivates the donors who fuel the mission? Are they moving in the same direction as the organization or have they rejected the organization's full mission?

Donors either center an organization on its full mission or contribute to Mission Drift. Despite this influence, only a very small percentage recognize the role they play.

But Greg is an exception.

"Hi, Peter, this is Greg. Hey, when you get a minute, would you give me a call? I have something I'd like to discuss with you."

As I listened to this voice mail, I could tell Greg had something important on his mind. It wasn't the words he used, but his tone that concerned me. This wasn't going to be a conversation just to catch up and laugh again about our experiences traveling together to the Dominican Republic and Haiti.

When I eventually reached him, he shared that he had some concerns about HOPE's messaging. Specifically, he recently watched an end-of-year video I made thanking our supporters. In it, I shared some of the important milestones we had crossed. I told the story of a family we served in Rwanda and how *our efforts* had impacted their lives. I wished everyone a merry Christmas and happy New Year. I thought it was okay.

But Greg disagreed. "Peter, this wasn't the full HOPE story."

Greg went on to describe how the Gospel was only peripherally mentioned. Watching the video for a second time, I saw he was right. The full message of HOPE was truncated to emphasize only the numerical highlights and *our* achievements. I missed the opportunity to communicate our full mission and properly give credit to God.

More than anyone else I know, Greg actively monitors the communication of organizations he supports. As a financial advisor with Morgan Stanley, he understands his role as an investor in ministries and takes his role seriously. Discontent to just write a check, Greg actively monitors his charitable investments. And this means he calls when he sees inconsistency.

Supporters of organizations have much more influence than they realize. If benefactors request clarity and consistency in messaging and implementing the mission, organizations respond. When I receive phone calls from people I respect who are investing in our organization, I pay close attention.

Twelve months later, we made another end-of-year thank-you video. As I prepared my brief remarks, I could hear Greg in the back of my mind urging accuracy in sharing our complete message.

Shortly after I pressed "send" on the email, I received another voice mail from Greg. This time, I recognized a very different tone in his voice.

"What a difference this year!" he celebrated.

Money is influence. Carnegie's philanthropy caused universities to sever all religious ties. Greg's philanthropy helps organizations stay true to their mission.

Long-Term Impact

It's easy to find stories about the power of funding and the way it contributes to Mission Drift. In this book, we've already highlighted several examples.

Financially supporting an organization makes you a stakeholder. It gives you influence. Do your homework and invest in causes in line with your beliefs. And question them if you see inconsistency or the seeds of Mission Drift. Every time you put a check in the mail you are sending a message: "Yes, I believe in what you are doing."

Don't be passive.

Bruce Konold, senior pastor of Eagan Hills Church, a Christian Missionary Alliance congregation in Eagan, Minnesota, said that he personally invests time in understanding the ministries he's partnering with.

"As a pastor, I need to personally invest time. . . . I can't delegate all of it out. There's no substitute for personally being acquainted with the organizations you support," said Bruce. "It sounds kind of silly, but I read several missionary newsletters each month."

When he sees an organization experiencing drift, Konold says that it is easier to just stop funding the organization, but he chooses to address the issue.

"We don't like to confront," Konold said. This is true both at church and with charitable organizations.

"If individuals are unhappy at church, they often don't address the issue. They just leave. It's the same with donors." Most donors would rather pull the funding than bring an issue to the forefront.

"We'd be far better off if we would have the courage to confront . . . and we would rather back away than deal with an issue," said Konold.[11] But a painful conversation can save an organization from taking another step away from their core identity.

Cliff Benson, desiring to support a Christ-centered school, created a Legacy Fund at the National Christian Foundation (NCF). Legacy Funds allow donors to clearly and thoroughly document their giving intentions. NCF ensures that their desires are carried out, even if they want their heirs involved in distributing some or all of the funds.

Cliff tied the fund to the mission of the Christian school. As long as the school remains distinctively Christian, it will receive funding, but if it ever drifts away from that mission, the funding stops. Cliff's hope is that the fund will become large enough to one day have the exact opposite effect of Carnegie's gift—keeping the school anchored in its Christian mission.

I'm thankful for individuals like Bruce, Cliff, and Greg who are bold enough to address organizations when they see warning signs of organizational drift. They understand their influence, and they seek to use it to keep organizations on mission.

Contingency Planning

At a luncheon in Houston with a group of astute and highly successful entrepreneurs, philanthropist David Weekley asked, "What steps have you taken to ensure your foundation stays on mission after you're gone?"

No hands raised. No comments. No examples to highlight. Even though their businesses had contingency planning, their personal foundations had not done anything to ensure that they would stay on mission. No one had documented their core beliefs and the types of missions and organizations they wanted to fund.

Yet, they could all give examples of Mission Drift. They all knew how often donor intent was ignored, much like the case of Howard Pew, as we highlighted in chapter 5. Why this disconnect between most philanthropists' understanding Mission Drift yet having done little to prevent it?

In follow-up conversations, it is clear there are multiple reasons for this disconnect. Most common was the belief that we will have more time. *It's important but not urgent, so why not put it off until later?* Unless we're surrounded by doctors and nurses or in hospice care, we have many other important projects to focus on. Life is busy. Besides, thinking about what happens when we're gone requires us to think about our own mortality—and that's just no fun.

Others commented that their spouse and kids know what they value and would keep future funding on mission.

But Roger Sandberg Sr. of the National Christian Foundation challenged this thinking by asking a simple question, "What was your great-grandfather's name and occupation?"[12]

I (Peter) paused—and tried to remember.

Given my slow response, Sandberg's point was already made.

If we can't even remember the name and occupation of our great-grandfathers, how would we know what they valued and what causes ignited their passions? How likely is it that future generations will continue supporting the causes we passionately believe in?

This issue isn't just for megaphilanthropists to consider. Each of us has the privilege of sharing what we value by being intentional with our support. We either create incentives for organizations to remain on mission, or we fuel their drift through our apathy.

Understanding our influence as donors is the first step toward effective Mission True giving, but the second step is perhaps even more important. We need not just to give, but to give with intentionality.

Generators and Sunsets

Financial author Ron Blue said to a group of philanthropists at Generous Giving, "Do your giving while you are living so you know where it is going."[13]

This approach, called sunsetting, means you set a date upon which all assets are given away. Rather than just giving a small percentage of the funds in perpetuity, sunsetters give with a clear end date. This enables them to see some of the impact of their gifts and also determine the causes they support.

Robert and Patricia Kern founded Generac Power Systems, one of the world's largest generator businesses. When they sold Generac for over one billion dollars in 2006,[14] the Kerns put most of these resources into their family foundation. The foundation gives away money in ways that "enrich the lives of others by promoting strong pastoral leadership, educational excellence and high quality, innovative engineering talent."[15]

The Kerns believe in sunsetting.[16] Their goal is to give away hundreds of millions of dollars over the next twenty years in order to avoid the potential generational issues associated with Mission Drift.

According to David Wills, president of the National Christian Foundation, an increasing number of people are sunsetting their personal wealth—giving more generously now and also setting a final date upon which all their remaining resources will be distributed.

Wills says, "There is so much work to be done and, at the same time, so much momentum in the taking of the whole Gospel to the whole world. There has never been a better time to be alive and experience the joy of taking what has been entrusted to impact others."[17]

Philanthropic Mentoring

Another way to ensure giving stays on target is to involve family in giving now. Whether they will be giving away wealth that is made available to them to give or they themselves are entrusted with more than they need, giving becomes an opportunity for discipleship and deepening relationships.

A generous philanthropist commented, "Donor intent begins in the cradle."[18] The key is to inculcate values in future generations and recognize the importance of modeling and mentoring in thoughtful generosity.

Thanksgiving in the Chrisman family is about much more than just turkey and pumpkin pie. It's a time to realize how much they have been truly blessed as a family and to give thanks to God. Each year, they provide $1,000 to each of their children to give to the charity of their choosing. They ask each child to research organizations and create a video describing where they gave the money and why as a Christmas present to their parents. In this way the entire family can truly give thanks and celebrate together.[19]

It's more than just celebrating Christmas and supporting causes; it's modeling how decisions are made and what common values the family holds. It's discipleship through the tool of generosity. Jesus celebrates thoughtful philanthropy. When the widow donates a small amount to the offering, Jesus lauds her commitment to sacrificial giving.[20] We should teach and model generosity for those around us.

After reading a draft of this book, philanthropist friends of ours wrote a simple, one-page summary of their values and philanthropic priorities. It's not a bulletproof strategy, but it provided an educational opportunity for them with their children. It gave their heirs crystal-clear guidance on their philanthropic vision and values and is a safeguard to prevent the type of grave reversal evidenced by the

Pew Charitable Trusts, as we outlined earlier in the book. Their giving charter is included in appendix 3.

Mission True Donors

Mission True organizations need donors who are with them. Encourage, challenge, and fund them with a spirit of generosity and humility. God can accomplish remarkable things through His people linking arms together to support important causes. Mission True donors:

1. *Are explicit in their expectations:* By creating clear guidelines and a plan for your giving, you "memorialize" your values and intent. Henry Crowell (founder of The Crowell Trust, profiled in chapter five) modeled this clarity through his indenture.
2. *Plan ahead:* It's morbid to consider, but thinking about your estate planning and bequests now will create an opportunity for you to have important conversations with your family.
3. *Keep "mission strings" attached:* Organizations like the National Christian Foundation can help to build safeguards around your giving. Their mission is to give billions of dollars to Christian ministries. They want to help you give well.
4. *"Do your giving while you're living"*[21]: The best way to avoid Mission Drift in your giving is to prayerfully give everything you can while you can still control where it goes.
5. *Pray for and encourage the organizations you love:* Our friendships with donors like Greg, Terry, and Cliff are some of the most life-giving relationships we hold. They are a constant encouragement to us and help us stay on mission. Embrace your role as a stakeholder, praying for and encouraging these organizations to stay Mission True.

Decision Points

After receiving the ultimatum from the foundation in Houston mentioned in chapter one, I responded in an email. I conveyed my appreciation for their past support. But I also communicated that it was simply impossible for us to water down our mission. That email ended our formal partnership.

But in the following years, the most remarkable thing happened. By sharpening our mission, we experienced a dramatic increase in support and grew rapidly. People who were fully in line with our mission stepped up to give even more generously. It turned out there were many supporters of microfinance who were passionate about spiritual impact. Since that decision, our annual revenue and number of donors have more than doubled.

Many Mission True organizations we've identified have also experienced growth as they have championed the cause of Christ. Inter-Varsity, Compassion, Youth For Christ, Taylor, National Christian Foundation, International Justice Mission, Young Life, and Cru have all seen dramatic increases in their charitable revenue over the past ten years, even through the Great Recession.

We don't think this a coincidence. The silent majority of donors believe in these organizations and want them to remain Mission True. Many individuals are willing to partner with you not *despite* your faith but *because* of it.

There's no guarantee that financial success will be the result of remaining Mission True. But even if funding runs out and you close your doors, is this not a better outcome than lasting while compromising on things most precious to you?

Ultimately, this becomes an issue of trust. Will God provide? Proverbs reminds us of the answer: "Trust in the Lord with all your heart and lean not on your own understanding; in all your ways submit to him, and he will make your paths straight."[22] If we believe fully in God—and trust His sovereignty—we will get to work and do all we can, but fully submit the results of our efforts to His divine plan.

And this is exactly what Nico did. Today, if you travel to his Eduplex school in South Africa, you will see a school, actually several schools: a preschool, a primary school, and now a high school. They were built without the Swiss funders' support. The school accomplished its mission without compromising its identity. Other supporters stepped up. In fact, during a trip to Switzerland, Nico received one of his largest donations from an individual who *only* gave because Nico's charity was strongly Christ-centered.

Funding is influence. It also provides tests to expose how much you value your full mission and if your identity is for sale. Mission True organizations not only link arms with like-minded donors, they also measure their success with metrics reflective of the entirety of their mission.

11

MEASURING
WHAT MATTERS

Mission True organizations track metrics
reflective of their full mission

Customer Service Legends

Nordstrom is known for its incredible customer service and high-performing sales staff. During business school, I (Chris) had the chance to visit the Nordstrom headquarters. While there, my cohort and I tried our best to discover Nordstrom's "secret sauce." We met with Jack McMillan, retired co-chairman at Nordstrom and a third-generation member of the Nordstrom family.

When we asked McMillan for their secrets, he responded bluntly, "It's all about the numbers."

McMillan explained the creative ways they track and celebrate individual sales performance. At the start of each day, they post a top-ten list in the back room, ranking the sales staff based on their previous day's sales. This sales culture has led Nordstrom to over 200 retail locations in 44 countries.

While the sales success of the organization was clear, what impressed me more than their high-performing culture were the framed customer letters lining the corridors. Letters from loyal Nordstrom fans who experienced the exceptional care of the Nordstrom team filled the hallways.

One of the customers wrote a gripping story about how she lost the diamond from her wedding ring while trying on clothes at Nordstrom. Three Nordstrom staff members scoured the floors, but couldn't find it. So they searched through all the filthy vacuum bags till they finally located it.

At a corporate board meeting, they highlighted the above-and-beyond gesture from the stage. The three employees were recognized publicly and brought on stage in front of the shareholders because of their extraordinary service.[1]

Measuring sales totals is easy. But how could Nordstrom measure remarkable customer service?

When McMillan described analyzing something as tricky and nuanced as customer care, he responded without pause. "Well, of course we track it. We look at the numbers."

Nordstrom managers solicit customer feedback and measure each employee's commitment to excellence in customer service. They celebrate and encourage handwritten notes and personal home deliveries, quantifying these thoughtful touches from their staff.[2] McMillan described how Nordstrom managers even track the number of interactions their security guards have with customers.[3]

Measuring the Nebulous

Nordstrom's heroic customer service has reached legend status. They are fodder for business school case studies and articles. An entire book has been devoted to *The Nordstrom Way to Customer Service Excellence*. *Fortune* magazine ranks Nordstrom in its Hall of Fame for best places to work.[4]

In our efficiency-crazed, multitasking, grab-a-Starbucks-venti-on-the-go age, this form of customer service seems almost archaic. It's surprising an organization like Nordstrom has survived.

But Nordstrom leaders believe the company is profitable *because* they track more than financial indicators. They measure their number-one goal, customer service. In itself, this measurement doesn't tell the entire Nordstrom story. But it captures the most important story.

As Nordstrom demonstrates, to achieve the full aim of your mission, you have to be deliberate in what you evaluate. Mission True organizations find a way of stating and measuring what they believe matters most, even something as "fuzzy" as outstanding customer service.

"What gets measured gets done" is a well-worn business mantra. And for good reason—it's true. But on the flip side, measuring the wrong things can just as easily lead an organization off mission.

Insufficient Celebrations

"We just gave our one millionth loan," I (Peter) proudly announced to our staff a couple years ago. "And this is a milestone worth celebrating!"

With a PowerPoint backdrop of histograms, we outlined where we'd been. We highlighted major numerical successes we'd experienced. We recognized the programs and people who went above and beyond in accomplishing these goals. We closed our time praying together. We even had brightly colored balloons and ate cake while we sent congratulatory notes to the overseas team members who weren't able to celebrate with us.

Many of our staff members are business minded and agree that crossing a major numerical milestone is worth celebrating. A couple weeks later at another staff meeting, a team member shared that eight individuals in Brazzaville had come to know Christ through our staff. I said an enthusiastic "Praise God!" But that was it.

Jesse, our vice president of administration, pulled me aside afterward. "We regularly celebrate the numerical milestones, but I wonder if we could do a better job celebrating when we see lives touched by Christ."

Whenever Jesse says, "I wonder . . ." I pay attention because it is always followed by a thoughtful suggestion I need to hear. He properly recognized that since Scripture tells us angels in heaven deem it worth celebrating when one person turns to Christ, it is worth us celebrating as well.

What Matters Most

It is natural to focus on easy-to-measure indicators: total donations, percent-to-program, and number of people served.

And these are important things to measure. Auditors, nonprofit evaluators, and the Better Business Bureau all need this data to hold us accountable and to benchmark against industry standards.

Though important, these indicators tell us nothing about the impact on the people we're serving or how well we're using the funds to accomplish our mission. Measuring just these indicators would be like a hospital measuring revenue, a few efficiency ratios, and the total number of patients served. Important institutional indicators, but they tell us nothing about the objective of the hospital: Are patients being cured?[5]

For a faith-based organization, a preoccupation with financial and growth metrics unintentionally sends the message that financial and numerical successes are preeminent.

What's *not* measured slowly becomes irrelevant.

This is an issue we've experienced firsthand. In our organization, our fascination with metrics has sometimes undermined our effectiveness and outreach. Ironically, it was shortly after this one millionth loan celebration that we uncovered significant operational lapses.

We were not built to last, and several of our international programs were clearly off mission. While the balloons from the party were still deflating, we realized we were in trouble, and yet many of our key performance indicators were telling us we were still successful.

It is possible to be successful in the things that ultimately don't matter to your organization's success.

Taking inventory of where we went wrong, we realized what we really measured, monitored, and celebrated was almost exclusively growth. If the charts were up and to the right, we were happy. More money raised and more families served. This is what drove us.

We passionately believe in our mission and believe growth is good, yet it can be terribly misleading because growth indicators say nothing about the *impact* of the growth or the *quality* of the outreach or institution. Focusing exclusively on growth can also cause organizations to pursue funding opportunities they know will pull them off mission. It can cause them to sacrifice quality. It can give the faulty impression that everything is being done well. It can lead to an inflated ego and a decreasing quality product. Using the wrong metrics can be a cause of Mission Drift.

Concerned about setting the wrong goals, my friend in Houston decided not to set any goals, but instead increased the emphasis on analyzing each deal. This allowed his company to be open to every opportunity without the pressure of some arbitrary goal that might cause them to make the wrong decision. The result: a return on investment superior to Warren Buffett's Berkshire Hathaway over the past fifteen years.

To remain on mission, we need a deeper definition of success and a more thoughtful approach to metrics. But we must start by recognizing that there is no perfect tool; all measurement is imperfect.

Conversion Counting

A nonprofit analyst recently told us of a survey he conducted in Haiti. As part of the survey, he collected newsletters from missionaries and ministries working throughout the country. And then he aggregated the number of people each organization reported coming to Christ. At the end of his research, he realized something shocking.

According to the data, the entire population of Haiti would be saved every three years! Clearly, something was wrong in how organizations were measuring and monitoring their impact.

All the organizations were trying to measure what mattered. They each believed they were doing the right thing. They each believed they were having a significant impact. Yet clearly the aggregated data just didn't make sense.

Meaningful monitoring and evaluation is more difficult than we may realize.

Desiring to learn about best practices in Mission True monitoring and evaluation, we recently sent staff to the Spiritual Metrics conference hosted by Eastern University and Global Scripture Impact (GSI). Representatives from leading Christian relief and development organizations came together to share what they've learned. Over three days, leading development experts gave presentations on the theology behind biblical planning and the importance of creating structures for stewardship. Topics discussed included: How do we stay faithful to mission through metrics? Are the ways we use metrics God-honoring? What are the various methods of measurement?

At each presentation, the group humbly shared that though they may have been marked as experts, few had been doing this for very long, and even with their minimal experience they had faced significant challenges in implementing the work.

The conclusion: No one has this figured out. But this should not mean we do not try.

In graduate school, one of my (Peter) favorite classes was on monitoring and evaluation with a senior economist at the World Bank. I enjoyed the class so much that I became a course assistant the following year and essentially retook the class.

One of the conclusions from two years in the class taught by Michael Woolcock, a leader in the field of international development and a wonderful person, is that even the massive entity of the World Bank seriously struggles with monitoring and evaluation. It was rather easy to find gaps in even the most rigorous assessment.

- How do you determine causality? Just because there is a positive impact on the people you served, how do you know it is the result of your services?
- Is there a true counterfactual, a way of measuring what would have happened in the absence of the intervention? Are you comparing against a group of people with the same characteristics?
- Was there observer bias? How do you know the respondents didn't act differently because of the person implementing the survey?
- How do you ensure it was a perfect random sample? Was there selection bias?
- What other methodological challenges stopped you from conclusively establishing causality?
- The list of challenges goes on.

I thought back on all the impact assessment studies I'd participated in, saw with new eyes the gaps in methodology, and realized nothing we had ever measured could be verified as undeniable "proof" of the impact of our services.

Instead of leading to paralysis or throwing our hands up, this realization can open us up to discovering the very best way we can monitor key metrics given current resources and constraints.

As Dave Larson, a development expert who participated in a United States Agency for International Development Survey study summarized, "Our goal should be to *improve* our services, not just *prove* the impact."[6]

When Close Enough Is Good Enough

Paul Penley, the director of research at the philanthropic advisory firm Excellence in Giving, has had a recurring conversation with ministry leaders over the years.

First, they acknowledge the need to measure outcomes.

"Then there is a pause," he said. "And the infamous contrastive conjunction 'but' begins the next statement."

Program leaders offer sincere excuses. They can't do metrics because they believe they are "the exception."[7]

Nordstrom proved they can measure nebulous activities. We can too. In his experience, Penley has found most ministries *can* develop an instrument—albeit imperfect—of measurement. And for an issue as important as this is, imperfect measurement is far better than no measurement at all.

So where do you begin?

"Measurement and mission go together in my book," shared Penley.

Beams strengthen a house's structure; similarly, the purpose of measuring outcomes is to reinforce the mission. When drafting assessments, organizations should measure ways to best advance the mission, as well as identify issues that could threaten it.

"The questions they are answering from data collected should tell me if they are solving the problem their mission says is central to their existence," said Penley. "If not, we've got a problem."[8]

As a starting point, Penley suggests organizations begin with the following yes-or-no questions as a self-analysis:

1. Have we translated our mission into specific and measurable goals?
2. Are we asking those we serve whether programs are effective and having impact?
3. Are we measuring program outcomes against benchmarks or averages?
4. Have we completed independent evaluation of program outcomes?
5. Do we use an internal scorecard to track key performance indicators?

Mission True organizations move beyond the paralysis of perfection and get to work measuring what matters most.

You Are What You Measure

A few years ago, Youth For Christ (YFC) recognized that what they measured was inadequate. Every week at chapels, kids were making confessions of faith, but a simple confession did not always result in a changed life. Altar-call metrics didn't indicate whether YFC's mission—"to raise up lifelong followers of Jesus"—was being fulfilled.

"We could do altar calls and get every kid to make a profession of faith in juvenile halls, for example," said Tim Skrivan, vice president at YFC. "But, our mission is about disciples, not professions [of faith]. We weren't seeing 'quality' in our metrics. We were measuring, but very passively."[9]

Characteristic of Mission True organizations, YFC had the humility to embrace a new model instead of rigidly clinging to the way things were always done.

They changed what they measured. Instead of measuring success by the number of students who confessed faith, YFC now intentionally tracks whether youth become active in local churches after their confessions of faith.

The Funnel of Kids We Reach in YFC: How We Measure Focused Ministry

		Impact Question #
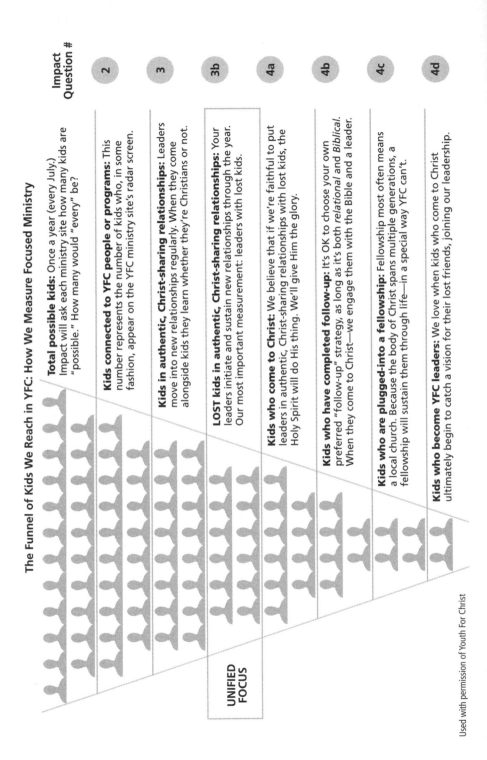	**Total possible kids:** Once a year (every July.) Impact will ask each ministry site how many kids are "possible." How many would "every" be?	2
	Kids connected to YFC people or programs: This number represents the number of kids who, in some fashion, appear on the YFC ministry site's radar screen.	3
	Kids in authentic, Christ-sharing relationships: Leaders move into new relationships regularly. When they come alongside kids they learn whether they're Christians or not.	3b
UNIFIED FOCUS	**LOST kids in authentic, Christ-sharing relationships:** Your leaders initiate and sustain new relationships through the year. Our most important measurement: leaders with lost kids.	
	Kids who come to Christ: We believe that if we're faithful to put leaders in authentic, Christ-sharing relationships with lost kids, the Holy Spirit will do His thing. We'll give Him the glory.	4a
	Kids who have completed follow-up: It's OK to choose your own preferred "follow-up" strategy, as long as it's both *relational* and *Biblical*. When they come to Christ—we engage them with the Bible and a leader.	4b
	Kids who are plugged-into a fellowship: Fellowship most often means a local church. Because the body of Christ spans multiple generations, a fellowship will sustain them through life—in a special way YFC can't.	4c
	Kids who become YFC leaders: We love when kids who come to Christ ultimately begin to catch a vision for their lost friends, joining our leadership.	4d

YFC wasn't afraid to transform their scorecard. Like many youth ministries, YFC relies on outside funding. And fundraising consumed the thoughts and decision making of their leaders. For some of their 160 chapters nationwide, up to 75 percent of their board meeting discussions centered on fundraising.

YFC decided to change the discussion and put a standardized ministry scorecard in front of every chapter to guide their thinking, planning, and strategy. For each data point they collect, they have a series of questions for board members and senior staff to work through. Some of the new things measured include:

- How many Christ-sharing relationships with kids are we in?
- How many leaders do we have in those relationships?

Their new scorecard helped them realign their focus at board meetings and moved the organization more closely toward their vision.

It's not a perfect tool, but the new scorecard is a powerful indicator. YFC knows their mission to "raise up lifelong followers of Jesus" hinges upon Christ-sharing relationships between mature Christian leaders and kids. Defining and tracking these new metrics aligns YFC's leaders toward their true north.

Keeping It Simple

Returning to the story mentioned earlier in which Jesse reminded us to more fully celebrate HOPE's whole mission, we have made simple changes to our monitoring and metrics.

We created a framework for our strategic plan and key performance metrics, which are always in the following progression: Christ-centered, quality, and then growth.

Our highest goal is to remain faithful to our Christ-centered identity and mission. Because of our identity, we must pursue excellence. Nothing undermines the message of Christ more quickly than a poor product—a matter we will explore further in the next chapter. If, and only if, we are living our Christ-centered mission and implementing it with excellence, will we focus on growth.

We attempt to curb the enthusiasm for growth by ensuring it is third on our list and follows faithfulness to our identity and operational excellence. Changing the order of what we celebrate has reoriented our perspective and had implications throughout the organization.

We also concentrate on truly celebrating more than just quantitative success. When we hear stories of changed lives in places around the world, we pick up the phone to share the good news. This small gesture makes the global team know that we care about more than just numerical growth.

In one country, staff members keep a logbook where they share stories of lives changed. Our leaders read these stories at staff meetings and the logbook becomes a journal of what we believe is truly success. It cost us a notebook, a pen, and a little time each week to implement. Stories don't prove impact, but rather remind employees of a key aspect of identity and purpose. And they are important to encourage our donors as well.[10]

More formally, Metrix Research Group created an assessment to measure four aspects of transformation, including:

- **Spiritual Restoration**—development of a right relationship with God leading to spiritual maturity, faith in action, and disciple making.

- **Personal Restoration**—the realization of God-given potential and purpose leading to a greater sense of self-worth and a brighter future.

- **Social Restoration**—reconciliation between people leading to a community characterized by solidarity, collaborative service, justice, respect, and interdependence.

- **Material Restoration**—economic transformation evidenced by self-sufficiency, financial stability, crisis management, and improved quality of life.

This tool tracks clients over time and compares veteran groups to new groups entering the program. In addition to measuring outputs, it explores whether values and attitudes are changing.

Are people more optimistic about the future? Are people growing in their relationship with Christ or more open to the claims of Jesus? Is our training effective in helping families work their way out of material poverty? Are people experiencing an improved quality of life? How do families served describe the influence of staff members on their lives? Are those we serve more charitable toward their communities?

This tool is imperfect. It will never prove beyond all doubt the impact of our programs. But it does help center HOPE around a very clear definition of success and give us important data beyond just whether or not fundraising revenue is growing.

Giving Credit Where Credit's Due

If you want to create measures of success beyond fundraising or numerical success, you need to be intentional about it. But you also need to have a healthy dose of humility.

Improving the way you measure your mission or implementing a ministry scorecard can provide a panoramic view of goals and dreams. These metrics keep the vision of the organization in front of you.

But we can never forget what Paul says in 1 Corinthians, "I planted the seed, Apollos watered it, but God has been making it grow."[11]

We need to remember that though we may plant seeds, others water them. No matter where your organization works, more than your organization alone plays a role. A constellation of institutions and people contribute toward success. It might be easy for a university to chart their students' spiritual growth, but the university alone is not responsible. Local churches, parachurch ministries, family, and friends play important roles in those students' lives.

Even more important, we must submit that God does the work. Growth and any success we achieve should simply fill us with gratitude for what God is doing. God is "making it grow."

Mission True Metrics

When metrics become like a victory platform where we pump our fists, we know we are headed in the wrong direction. Metrics can serve to puff us up and glorify our efforts, rather than glorifying the One who originates all good things. Mission True organizations:

1. *Make an effort to measure more than just the "easy" stuff:* For their donors, staff, and board, demonstrating holistic success really matters.
2. *Identify ways measurement can lead them off mission:* They recognize how poor prioritization or shallow data might lead them to wrong conclusions and result in drift.
3. *Believe measuring something is better than nothing:* When it comes to matters of the heart, Mission True organizations recognize they must track something to keep their hearts and minds focused on the entirety of their mission.
4. *Admit it's a team effort:* They do not use metrics to toot their measurement horns. They measure with open hands, acknowledging their dependence on God and others for their success.

Dallas Willard reminds us of a bigger picture we need to remember when we approach monitoring and measurement: "Vision of God secures humility. Seeing God for who he is enables us to see ourselves for who we are."[12]

Metrics can be self-serving. We need to be clear on *why* we pursue them. Is it to improve services or bolster marketing materials? Is it to hold us to our mission or to use as a bully stick to show that we're better than our peer organizations?

Seeing God for who He is clarifies our role: We are stewards. Metrics help us to remain accountable for the work that God has placed in our hands. Mission True organizations are fixated on stewardship. And it's because of this stewardship they recognize a haunting reality—mediocrity could undermine everything.

12

Etched in Excellence

Mission True organizations understand the
Gospel demands excellence in their work

In an aging office building in a small Romanian town, Dorian[1] articulated a troubling reality about his organization: Nobody liked it.

I (Chris) was in Romania to find a potential microfinance partner organization for HOPE. We already had a presence in Ukraine, Russia, and Moldova, so a generous donor encouraged us to consider expanding into neighboring Romania. We agreed it would be a great locale for expansion.

Peter picked me to conduct the feasibility study at the start of 2007. Because who doesn't love traveling, basically, to the Siberian Tundra in the dead of winter? I'm still not sure if it was a promotion or a demotion, but I accepted the challenge and proceeded to the former Communist nation with long underwear and parka in tow.

While in Eastern Europe, I crisscrossed the region by train, meeting with dozens of leaders to learn about the needs of entrepreneurs and to examine the resources currently available. I met leaders of a number of microfinance organizations, both faith based and secular.

My final meeting was with Dorian, the executive director of a faith-based microfinance organization.

Dorian's organization provided business training, loans, and consulting services to Romanian entrepreneurs. But during our conversation, Dorian aired many grievances about the entrepreneurs they served throughout the country. While his ministry wanted to help them, it was as if they weren't interested in being helped.

When they offered biblically based business training sessions, no entrepreneurs would show up. When they issued business loans, very few paid them back. When they offered consulting services, nobody was buying. All their metrics—client growth, repayment rates, numbers of active church partners, etc.—were bad and getting worse.

Their entrepreneurs (and potential entrepreneurs) didn't value Dorian's organization. The more I learned, the clearer the picture became. It wasn't that Romanians had a personal vendetta against this organization. But it was like a baker who couldn't bake. This organization, quite simply, had poorly designed the financial products and training for the entrepreneurs they hoped to serve.

This would normally prompt sympathy from me, not frustration. But I felt more of the latter because of his closing remarks: "We're sad nobody is showing up for our training sessions or paying back their loans, but you know, we're telling them about Jesus," Dorian said. "And that's all that truly matters."

Ichthus-Washing

Mission True organizations affirm, reinforce, and celebrate their Christian distinctiveness. And Dorian's organization was certainly distinctively Christian in some ways. Dorian's comments contained a semblance of truth. I believe wholeheartedly that we need to share Jesus with those we serve. I believe our Christian distinctiveness is the very thing our world so desperately needs. If that hasn't been clear thus far in the book, we have really missed the mark. And in that light, Dorian's enthusiasm for the Gospel is admirable. But that's where my agreement with him stops.

Mission True organizations realize Christian distinctiveness involves more than boards, hiring, culture, and staff. It demands distinctiveness in the quality and effectiveness of their programs and operations. The Gospel must saturate the actual work we do. It must alter and shape both what we do and how we do it.

Dorian spoke as if creating a substandard product was honoring to God simply because of the words he spoke. He acted as though his organization shined simply because it featured a strong proclamation of the Gospel message. But the words spoken by this organization were undermined by the low quality of their work. Slapping an ichthus (the Christian fish symbol of the early church) on product packaging does not mean it honors God.

Christian shoddy is still shoddy.

"The Christian shoemaker does his Christian duty not by putting little crosses on the shoes," wrote Martin Luther, "but by making good shoes, because God is interested in good craftsmanship."[2]

Dorian decorated his organization with "little crosses." But it was a shallow and short-sighted perspective. We serve a God who created an earth that holds its axis and planets that hold their orbits. God articulated a breathtaking and precise blueprint for His tabernacle. And our God instructs us to do likewise, commanding we do our work with excellence.

The Rocky Mountains and the diverse wildlife of the Serengeti communicate the grandeur of God's handiwork. His design for the temple illustrates God's concern for details. When we ignore the needs of our customers, treat them with disdain, and "ichthus-wash" our products with spirituality, we do not reflect or honor our Creator.

In Mission True organizations, quality must be nonnegotiable. We saw this manifest beautifully in Post Falls, Idaho.

The Pastoral Craftsman

Flowing through the densely wooded mountains of northern Idaho and Washington, the Spokane River embodies the quintessential North-west. Along its journey, the river passes through the small town of Post Falls, Idaho. Renowned for outdoor recreation, Post Falls is the perfect home for Buck Knives.

The Buck Knives headquarters towers above the banks of the Spokane River. The company has achieved unparalleled success in their industry. Like Kleenex, Buck Knives aren't just *a* brand. They are *the* brand. Buck Knives is the country's most prominent knife company, with three hundred employees crafting upwards of five million knives annually.

On my twelfth birthday, my dad presented me (Peter) with a Buck knife. Hands down, this was the most memorable gift of my childhood. The wooden handle and the weight of the knife spoke of the quality materials. That knife was my constant companion on many outdoor adventures as I unknowingly continued in a very long and rich history of people who held a Buck knife.

In 1902, Hoyt Buck forged his first knife when he was just thirteen years old. Unrelentingly meticulous, even at a young age, Hoyt believed deeply that his Christian faith demanded he approach his work with excellence, "as to the Lord."[3]

Hoyt was a pastor, tinkering with knife making on the side. When America entered World War II in 1941, there was a call for weapon donations for American soldiers. In that moment, he made a decision to become bi-vocational.

And Buck Knives Was Born

Hoyt later shared, "I didn't have any knives [to offer], but I sure knew how to make them."[4] Hoyt bought an anvil, grinder, and a forge and crafted over 2,000 knives out of the basement of his church to donate to American soldiers.

The notoriety of Hoyt Buck's knives grew dramatically during World War II. And, after consistent prodding from close friends, Hoyt and his son, Al, purchased more equipment and began commercially producing knives. H.H. Buck & Son made about five knives daily through the 1940s.

Al's son Chuck Buck—truly a great name—is the chairman of Buck Knives today. He exudes warmth, and he's generous in every sense of the word.

"In the early days, my dad did the handle work and my grandpa did the blade work," Chuck shared. "Even when my grandpa was in the hospital, he still did the blade work from the hospital. Eventually, my grandpa figured my dad needed to learn how to make blades. My dad would go into the hospital every night until my grandpa was satisfied that he could make the blades just right."[5]

Hoyt Buck's adherence to quality is melded into the company he founded. Over one hundred years after he made his first knife, the Buck family is still zealously committed to quality and to Christian principles.

Growing from a company that produced a handful of knives to over 10,000 daily—without losing the commitment to quality—is a testament to Hoyt, Al, and Chuck's shared perspective on what it takes to run a company the right way.

While Buck knives are sold to the police and the American military, they're most heralded in one industry: Buck knives are a near mandatory companion for hunters in our country. The Buck folding lockblade knife—Model 110—is the gold standard. And regardless of the knife company, all folding lockblades are called "buck knives."

The Model 110's sturdy blade, simple design, and flawless fabrication are hallmarks of Buck knives. And because the Buck family holds such confidence in the quality of the craftsmanship, they personally guarantee every Buck knife for life. Accompanying the lifetime guarantee in the box is a simple message to the new knife buyer from the Buck family:

> If this is your first Buck knife, "Welcome aboard." You are now part of a very large family. We think of each one of our users as a member of the Buck Knives family. Now that you are family, you might want to know a little more about us. The fantastic growth of Buck Knives, Inc. was no accident. From the beginning, we determined to make God the Senior Partner. In a crisis, the problem was turned over to Him, and He hasn't failed to help us with the answer. Each knife must reflect the integrity of management. If sometimes we fail on our end, because we are human, we find it imperative to do our utmost to make it right. If any of you are troubled or perplexed and looking for answers, may we invite you to look to Him, for God loves you.
>
> Chuck Buck, Chairman/Owner of Buck Knives

> *"For God loved the world so much that He gave His only son; so that anyone who believes in Him shall not perish but have eternal life."—John 3:16*

Customers buying Buck knives hail from all corners of the world. From all faith backgrounds, tens of millions of people—from Shanghai to Moscow to San Antonio—own Buck knives and have read this simple Gospel message. The Bucks believe that the quality of their craftsmanship is crucial to validate this message. A substandard knife would undermine the message they include in the box.

Excellence Is Not Negotiable

Propelled by their faith, Buck Knives and many Mission True organizations are setting the standard for professional excellence. Unlike Dorian, they understand the inherent link between the services they provide and the way people hear their message. They are focused on letting their "light shine before others, that they may see your good deeds and glorify your Father in heaven."[6] Light doesn't shine when it comes packaged in an inferior product.

Mission True organizations not only hold themselves to the highest of standards because of their Christian identity, but they also recognize the contributions they are uniquely able to make to the world because of the advantages of being faith-based. Consider the following few examples of excellence:

- Taylor University has been ranked number one in the category of Best Regional Colleges for five years in a row by *U.S. News & World Report*.
- Recognizing the increase in bullying, Youth For Christ created an anti-bullying program and was invited to deliver it in public schools across the country because of the success of its initial implementations.
- Compassion International sponsors more children than almost any child sponsorship organization in the world.
- Prison Entrepreneurship Program has demonstrated a dramatic decrease in the recidivism rate after assisting ex-convicts with business training, dramatically decreasing the tax burden.
- Achieving significant scale and efficiency through partnership with The Chalmers Center and local churches, our church-based

savings and credit associations operate at less than 25 percent of the cost of secular programs funded by the Gates Foundation.

- Project 1.27, an adoption ministry founded by Colorado Community Church, has helped 243 foster children find "forever homes" with Christian families in eight years. Legislators and church leaders from across the country have invited Project 1.27 leaders to help them launch similar church-based initiatives to alleviate the pressures on the foster care system.[7]

These examples are just the beginning. In our research, we consistently heard statistics akin to these across industries, sectors, and contexts. It didn't matter if it was a foundation, urban ministry, school, adoption agency, or some other type of organization; many Christian faith-based organizations outperformed their secular peers *because of* their Christian identity.

It's easy for Mission True organizations to assume their secular counterparts have the market cornered on excellence. But when the president of one the most prestigious nonprofits in the world laments his organization's drift from its Christian heritage, we should take note.

Returning to the Roots

In these circumstances, universities, including Harvard, need to think hard about what they can do in the face of what many perceive as a widespread decline in ethical standards. . . . Several studies have found that undergraduates are growing less altruistic and more preoccupied with self-serving goals.[8]

Derek Bok, president at Harvard University from 1971–1991, penned these words in his annual letter to the Harvard Board in 1987. He sounded the alarm in this report, acknowledging several uncomfortable trends at his university.

Compared to graduates from earlier years, Harvard students cheated more and served their communities less. Students were less concerned about finding a "meaningful philosophy of life." Bok wrote about a moral decay unfolding in the lives of Harvard's students. Why the decay? Bok wrote a thirty-five-page letter to answer that question.

"Harvard was founded to prepare ministers of upright character," Bok shared, as he reflected on the history of his university. Harvard's founders created the school with this mission: "To be plainly instructed and consider well that the main end of your life and studies is to know God and Jesus Christ."

This was Harvard's reason for existing. But Derek Bok acknowledged the obvious: Harvard had lost sight of its founding mission. And there were dire consequences on its effectiveness because of it.

Pressed with growing concerns about the product of his institution—Harvard graduates—Derek Bok became a historian of his university. He unearthed the founding documents and studied the school in its earliest days. He attempted to reconcile "Harvard 1636" with "Harvard 1986."

Bok outlined how Harvard's leaders placed very high value on the moral development of their students during the 1700s and 1800s. They responded to student infractions like vandalism, drunkenness, and sexual misconduct with resolute seriousness. They emphasized character and urged students to live "god-fearing, upright lives."

In their hiring practices, Harvard hired first for mission fit. When interviewing faculty members, they looked preeminently at character, well before examining academic credentials. The curriculum and extracurricular content included Christian worldview training, promoted a "sacred regard for truth," and emphasized the study of virtues.[9]

But as time passed, these commitments began to shift.

Crumbling Foundation

"Despite the labor invested in this moral enterprise," Bok lamented, "the edifice began to crumble as the nineteenth century wore on."

During the late nineteenth century, Darwin's *On the Origin of Species* ushered in a "new intellectual environment." The bifurcation of science and faith created schisms within universities. Objectivity trumped religion, and the Christian convictions of Harvard's past presidents became "more and more quaint and out of joint with the academic spirit of the age."

The establishment of state schools also infused a "more secular attitude" toward higher education. Soon, the university's strong faith heritage and commitment to character development "fell into disfavor."

Harvard's approach to hiring shifted, as we documented in chapter nine. Discipline changed on campus. The training of "mind and
character was separated" and the moral codes and campus chapel
programs were forever altered. Harvard's educational imperatives
narrowed in on technical training and academic rigor alone, abandoning the softer and less scientific domains like ethics, virtue, and faith.

By World War II, Harvard's moral vision had "largely evaporated."
A study of 1964 and 1965 Harvard graduates concluded with a depressing note: "The college had relatively little lasting effect on [gradu-
ates'] moral and ethical views." Bok knew the very foundation of the
enterprise of higher education was cracking at the seams.

Harvard is the benchmark against which all universities are measured, but even its president mourned Harvard's Mission Drift. When
one of the largest and most influential nonprofit organizations in the
world acknowledges the seriousness of their own drift—and their
lack of excellence in their products, the students—there are lessons
for Mission True organizations to learn.

Bok ended the report with a few recommendations, strategies for
helping students "acquire concern for others," a new code of conduct,
revised "ethical standards," and a suggestion for increased emphasis
on character in hiring staff and faculty members.

Near the end of his letter, Bok clarified his remarks to ensure that
his readers understood he was not suggesting Harvard return to its
historic roots. "Particular religious doctrines, however important
they may be in guiding the ethical beliefs of individual students, can
never be adopted by a secular university as the basis for its program
of moral education."[10]

It is this caveat that undermines the credibility of his recommendations. Appealing to an undefined, ethereal set of universal values
is not possible when there is no bedrock or standard of truth. There
is no values-neutral worldview capable of accomplishing these aims.
Secularism attempts to create a moral framework, yet it lacks the
foundational grounding required to make a framework that's durable
and lasting.

This is why Bok's recommendations twenty years ago have had marginal (if any) influence on the problems he identified. A guiding policy of tolerance and secularism, without any foundation, results in no change.

Today, Harvard boasts "debauchery" parties providing guests with condom door prizes.[11] One Harvard dorm hosts Incest-Fest, where nothing is off-limits.[12] And a provocative student newspaper made national headlines by including nude pictures of students.[13] Administrators accept the students' "freedom" to express themselves however they choose.

Mission True Organizations

Mission True organizations integrate the Gospel into their programs holistically. Whether providing microfinance services to Romanian entrepreneurs, forging knives, or educating students, they understand that the Gospel should reorient the work we do. Mission True organizations:

1. *Maintain the highest levels of quality:* "Poor quality" and "Christian" should never be used to describe the same organization. Substandard work runs contrary to God's calling. Unlike Dorian's organization, they "work at it with all [their] heart, as working for the Lord, not for human masters."[14]

2. *Celebrate their unique societal contributions because of their Christian identity:* They embrace their Christian distinctiveness and laud the ways this gives them unique opportunities in the places where they work.

3. *Integrate the Gospel into all areas of their programs:* There is no corner of the organizations where their Christian faith does not reach. Their products, services, policies, physical spaces, and strategies are oriented and framed by the Gospel.

When Hoyt Buck forged knives in the basement of his church, he routinely scrapped his progress and started from scratch if the quality of a given knife fell short of his standards. He was unwilling to etch the Buck name into a knife until it exceeded his very high expectations.

What would it look like if Christians exhibited that same level of quality control in our schools, urban ministries, and missions agencies? Dare we hold the bar that high? Are we willing to start from scratch when our work falls short? Or, like Dorian, do we believe that substandard—or even average—work is excused as long as Jesus' name is proclaimed?

Excellence undergirds Mission True companies. They understand that their mission is too important to settle for mediocrity. Our faith demands we lead "best in class" organizations, regardless of what type of work we do.

If our universities lag behind our secular counterparts, producing low-grade results and obtaining insufficient academic credentials, this does not bring honor to God. If our medical clinics need to apologize to patients for the underwhelming quality of care, we cloud the message we hope to share.

Distinctively Christian organizations hold extraordinary potential because of their faith convictions. Their firm worldview, belief in serving the needs of the whole person, and willingness to engage in murky topics of values and faith give them a leg up on their secular counterparts. But if that advantage is not stewarded well, it can weaken the work of us all. Mission True organizations are etched in excellence. Their programs—the work they do—must model the highest of quality.

But so must the "insides" of our organizations through a vibrant culture.

13

CULTURE EATS STRATEGY FOR BREAKFAST

Mission True organizations are fanatics
about rituals and practices

A crowd of rowdy college men guided blindfolded freshmen to an
unknown destination. The leaders hooted and hollered. The newly
arrived freshmen's minds raced with emotions, nervous about the
orientation their older peers had in store.

As they weaved through campus, the testosterone-laden pack became like a mob. The upperclassmen led with bravado, ratcheting up
the intensity of the initiation ceremony. They soon arrived at their
destination—the lake at the edge of campus. You might think you
know what happened next . . . but this wasn't your stereotypical college hazing.

The seniors sat the freshmen down on benches on a deck next to the
lake. They pulled off the blindfolds, but the freshmen weren't greeted
with beer cans or humiliating dares. J. R. Briggs was on one of those
benches as a freshman at Taylor University in 1997.

"All the seniors were there with buckets," Briggs reflected. "And they took our socks and shoes off and washed our feet. And then they hugged us and said, 'Welcome.'"[1]

Where embarrassing rituals and debauchery often reign, these seniors welcomed Briggs and his fellow freshmen with a foot-washing ceremony. This upside-down hazing is one small ritual experienced by one small slice of first-year Taylor students. But these small practices hold large importance.

Peter Drucker, one of the greatest management voices in history, said, "Culture eats strategy for breakfast."

Mission True organizations get this. They focus on the little things. They understand how important practices and norms are to the living and breathing cultures of their organizations. The small decisions each and every day may seem inconsequential, perhaps even trivial, but these little things protect against Mission Drift.

Animating the Bylaws

Corporate culture is tough to pin down. It's difficult to define. But it sure is easy to feel. As a rudimentary definition, culture is just "what happens." It's what you feel. It's how an organization practices its values and bylaws.

Culture predicts behavior. Embedded in the rites and rituals, culture takes a life of its own: It's just what an organization does.

And it's too important to leave to chance. As management consultant David Friedman said, "Authoring an organization's culture is a key aspect of quality leadership."[2]

In many ways, leaders cultivate corporate culture within faith-based organizations just like they cultivate their own spiritual lives. Spiritual disciplines create cadences and structures for our relationship with God to flourish. Likewise, in marriage, everyday rituals protect and sustain our relationship. Date nights, hand-holding, and shared prayer compose the rhythms of healthy marriages.

"Anyone who has mastered a golf swing or a Bach fugue is a ritual animal: one simply doesn't achieve such excellence otherwise," shared scholar James K. A. Smith. "In both cases, ritual is marked by *embodied repetition*. Ritual recruits our will through our body: the cellist's fingers become habituated by moving through scale after scale; the golfer's whole body is trained by a million practice swings. Because we are embodied creatures of habit—God *created* us that way—we are profoundly shaped by ritual."[3]

This is true for organizations as well.

Take two comparable companies: Southwest Airlines and United Airlines. On the surface, these two domestic air giants look alike. They are almost identical in size and scope. But any frequent flyer knows how stark the chasm is between these two.

Southwest consistently ranks among the top airlines in customer surveys. Southwest flight attendants are funny, engaging, and customer oriented. United Airlines, in contrast, consistently ranks at the bottom of all domestic airlines, recently dubbed in a customer survey as the "meanest airline."[4]

No one factor causes Southwest to have better customer service than United Airlines. Staffing, technology, and investor sentiment all influence the gap between Southwest and United. But Southwest's rituals, practices, and norms reinforce their mission statement: "Dedication to the highest quality of customer service delivered with a sense of warmth, friendliness, individual pride, and company spirit."

For me (Chris), the Southwest mission statement is more than nice words. I felt it.

Forging a Company Culture

On the front end of a donor trip from Denver, Colorado, to the Dominican Republic last year, I planned a one-day stopover in Philadelphia. Because the first leg of my flight from Denver to Philadelphia was domestic, I used my driver's license to board. Upon arriving in Philadelphia, however, I had a haunting realization: I did not have my passport.

With my flight to the Dominican Republic departing in twenty-four hours, I was in a bind.

After panicking for a few minutes, I scrambled for a solution. Because the donor trip was just three days in duration, I simply could not miss my departing flight. I didn't have any margin to postpone my flight, but I also didn't have an obvious way of getting my passport.

I explored catching a quick out-and-back flight to Denver to scoop up my passport, but the flight schedules were prohibitive. I then looked to see if my wife, Alli, could fly out to bring me my passport, but all the flights from Denver were full. FedEx couldn't overnight it. UPS Air was out too.

I explored option after option, but I came up empty each time. So I next called United, the airline taking me to the Dominican Republic. I thought they might have a flight attendant who could transport the passport to me. *Not possible*, they shared. *Against policy.* I prepared myself to call the donors to inform them of my embarrassing mistake. And to let them know the trip had to be canceled.

With nowhere else to turn, I reached out to the one company I thought might take a risk: Southwest. They had no incentive to help me. I wasn't an "A-List" card carrier (though I am now, partially because of their customer service heroism). I wasn't even booked on their airline to the Dominican Republic.

But when Alli showed up at their ticket counter in Denver, they responded as if her request was akin to asking to borrow a pen. They didn't hesitate to give her a special pass to get back to the gate. They alerted their flight attendants on the last flight out of Denver to Philadelphia. They (literally) cheered Alli on as she bolted from the ticket counter to security and through to the gate.

Alli arrived as the last passengers boarded. Out of breath and hoping against hope that our only remaining option would work, Alli made a smooth handoff. The flight attendant pocketed the passport and gave Alli confidence it would be delivered with care.

When I arrived at the Philadelphia airport the next morning, I approached the Southwest baggage claim office with trepidation. Everything hinged on Southwest—the flight attendant Alli handed my passport to, the Philadelphia nighttime desk worker who received the passport from the flight attendant, and then the morning crew. My trip depended on an unknown team.

And there it was. The baggage claim agent handed me an envelope— "Horst passport"—scribbled on the front. I ripped open the envelope, thumbed open to the first page, and saw my awkward passport photo looking back at me. I never thought I would be so happy to see my forced half-smile and creepy blank stare.

As I reflected on this whole ordeal, Southwest's heroism was not what impressed me most. It was the everyday nature of caring for customers that the Southwest employees exhibited. For them, this was an easy decision.

Much like Nordstrom, Southwest cares for their customers: That's culture.

Their people were empowered to make good decisions. They've ritualized it. When saving an absent-minded traveler—and preserving an important donor trip to the Dominican Republic in the process—is a "norm," you know you're doing something very right.

When the Office Pauses

International Justice Mission inspires us. Across the world, they shut down brothels, unchain girls trapped in the sex trade, assist in the creation and enforcement of laws to protect the vulnerable, and push back the worst sorts of darkness.

These freedom fighters enter into places of deep brokenness. But IJM realizes their workers cannot be sustained by their own gumption.

Last fall, our executive team visited the IJM executive team. During our time with them, we witnessed the underpinning of their life-changing work: daily prayer.

When we walked into their offices outside of Washington, D.C., the headquarters reflected the ethos of the company. Staff members dressed professionally. Ties, suits, and determination adorned the professionals walking throughout the office suite. Meetings started on time, and conference rooms were well equipped.

IJM means business.

But IJM's professionalism makes 11 a.m. at IJM all the more remarkable. Because at 11 a.m. each day, laptops close and phones go silent. The entire office—hundreds of employees—stops.

For thirty minutes each day, the entire IJM team prays together. They stop to surrender their efforts to God's provision. Staff accountants, executives, and marketers turn off their electronics and lift their voices to the great Healer and Provider. To the Lord who knows the names and deepest pains of every child slave. They bend their knees to Jesus, acknowledging it is God alone who makes their work possible.

"[Prayer is] not so much a matter of discipline, but a matter of desperation," extolled Gary Haugen, president and CEO of IJM. "Sometimes we get tired of praying, we forget to, or we simply don't want to."[5]

But even in those moments, they pray.

IJM's commitment to corporate prayer extends beyond their staff and clients. It even stretches into their relationships with their donors. Every year, the IJM team hosts donors and volunteers from across the world at their Global Prayer Gathering. Together, they dedicate their work to God. They submit their plans and brothel-eradicating efforts to Christ.

Prayer forges the culture of International Justice Mission. Prayer anchors their freedom fighters and opens doors human hands cannot.

A Surprisingly Dysfunctional Workplace

I (Chris) have two friends who recently quit their jobs at a nonprofit fighting human trafficking, an organization whose work resembled IJM's. They worked there for a few years. Drawn by the organization's unabashed Christ-centeredness and commitment to work with the poorest of the poor, they both traded potentially lucrative salaries to work what amounted to minimum-wage jobs for this mission.

They entered the jobs with bold expectations and enlivened spirits. But the organization squashed their expectations and enthusiasm. Quickly.

"The best word I can use to describe the work environment is *oppressive*," one of these friends shared. "There was no trust."

This organization engaged in remarkable poverty fighting work. And, as Christians, my friends resonated with the values of their employer. But what they found on the inside was not compelling. It was depressing.

The organization promised to save the world but trampled their employees in the process. After trying for a few years to make it work, my friends both threw in the towel. Tired of seeing colleagues chewed up and spit out by the toxic corporate culture, they quit. The culture sapped the very vibrancy from its employees who joined the organization because of its mission.

Behind the slick web site, its leaders created a divisive environment. Staff turnover rates soared. In my friends' short tenures there, they saw nearly a complete turnover of the staff.

Closed-door meetings were common. Hushed tones and secrecy wafted through the headquarters. Executive leaders sent conflicting messages to the staff. Leaders shrouded their remarks about the financial state of the organization. It was normal for junior staffers to gather secretly in hallways to pray for the organization and the constant state of disarray and distrust simmering in the office.

This organization's leaders created a culture of suspicion and panic. Their mission was compelling, but their internal reality was far from it. A cultural malaise infected the organization and might end up collapsing it, despite the profound nature of the anti-poverty work they're advancing.

Beyond Policies

Culture cannot be fully contained in an employee manual—but that is not to say that policies do not matter. Mission True organizations understand that policies reflect culture and underlying organizational values.

With Southwest, the staff members who showed a gracious response to a stranded traveler were not breaching policy. Rather, they were following policies and procedures created to enable sufficient flexibility to show outrageous customer service. The culture is integrated into the policies themselves.

LifeChurch.tv in Oklahoma City, a megachurch with a culture of excellence and professionalism, understands this tension. With thousands of children attending church at their campuses every weekend, Cathi Linch, treasurer, explains the need for guiding policies and processes such as their physical injury incident reporting form. But as simple as it sounds, the first procedure in the document is to "care for the injured person."

Their policies and processes are in place because they must conform to regulations, comply with insurance requirements, and appropriately manage risk. But their culture dictates that the "care for the injured person" is the highest value when responding to injury.

They create policies that help them more actively love their neighbors.

Little Is Big

Beyond policies, Mission True organizations recognize that culture is composed of all the "little things."

- The Crowell Trust trustees read aloud the charter of their foundation at the start of board meetings.
- Taylor University gives towels, along with diplomas, to its graduates, to signify the servant leadership of foot washing.
- Young Life has new staff members sit with storied leaders to learn the history of their organization.
- Jobs for Life puts a high level of trust in their regional staff members. They have high expectations and set ambitious goals, but they give flexibility to their team in how they accomplish them. In the process, they eschew the type of micromanaging that makes work miserable.
- InterVarsity reviews their vision statement piece-by-piece at their annual leadership conference. They exegete their values to a granular level, working hard to define and reinforce their shared identity.

"Culture is a balanced blend of human psychology, attitudes, actions, and beliefs that combined create either pleasure or pain, serious momentum or miserable stagnation," shared business consultant Shawn Parr. "A strong culture flourishes with a clear set of values and norms that actively guide the way a company operates."[6]

Mission True culture doesn't just happen. Thoughtful leaders intentionally craft the culture of their organizations and know it is too important to delegate. They create, reinforce, and celebrate the traditions and practices undergirding the culture. Ignoring the little things will mean drastic consequences in the long run, because a culture without purpose and intentionality will leave no defense against drift.

Drift is inevitable for organizations not anchored in a healthy and values-driven culture. And we don't need to look beyond a popular T-shirt company to see it.

Toxic T-Shirts

Tired of seeing American manufacturing jobs shipped overseas, Dov Charney created a new clothing company in 1997. He forged his ideals in the very name of his business: American Apparel.

The concept captured the imagination of young people. They adorned themselves with deep V-neck T-shirts and retro workout pants. American Apparel grew from Charney's side project to one of the nation's largest clothiers, grossing over $500 million in revenue in 2012.

For hipness-minded young people, the clothes are symbolic of American Apparel's culture: American-made and not-corporate. American Apparel is more than a brand. It is a statement.

But while cool kids mob the modern stores, a slow fissure grows in the home office. What started as a fun culture evolved into a *let loose* culture. And that evolved into today's American Apparel, a company encumbered by sexual discrimination lawsuits and a hostile work environment.

Once named Ernst & Young's Entrepreneur of the Year, Charney defines the American Apparel culture. He is brusque, consistently pushing the boundaries of appropriateness. His company's ads often land him in disputes with the Advertising Standards Authority in the U.K. because of their vulgar content. And he has been sued by at least eight different female employees because of his alleged moral misconduct.

Dubbed the "Hugh Hefner of retailing," Charney lauds his company's use of "sexually charged visual and oral communications in its marketing and sales activity."[7] He has been known to conduct board meetings in his underwear and frequently refers to his female colleagues with profanity.[8]

On the brink of bankruptcy several times, Charney has managed to keep American Apparel's operations afloat, but not without sinking his company's reputation in the process. The lead battering ram destroying his company's reputation is Charney, specifically the way his language and actions create a toxic culture.

Keith Miller, a board member at American Apparel, describes Charney's reputation as "a double-edged sword. As much as it can be tremendously value added, it is equal in erosion."[9]

Robert Johnston, associate editor at men's fashion magazine GQ, said,

> [Charney] comes over as such a sleazeball. Because their campaigns are slightly grubby, and he's more than slightly grubby, it all conspires to be rather unappealing. The whole image of American Apparel was supposed to be: "Aren't we good, making everything in the US and not using sweatshop labor?" Yet every story you hear about Dov himself is so sleazy that all the goodwill their ethical values should create is squandered. His reputation would certainly make me think twice before shopping there.[10]

On the surface, Charney is just an edgy provocateur. But *Fast Company* magazine says American Apparel's culture is "based on self-centered perversity."[11] Whether it's our friends' anti-poverty nonprofit or a pioneering clothier, the mission doesn't matter if your culture reeks.

Walkable Culture

I (Chris) recently returned to Taylor University, my alma mater, in rural Indiana. I walked by my dorm, Morris Hall, and then over to the Kesler Student Activities Center. From there, I wound back past my wife's dorm, Olson Hall. These stately brick buildings hold rich memories from my four years at Taylor.

But the buildings hold more than memories. They hold the legacy of the institution. They communicate stories of the people who embody Taylor's values. Samuel Morris, Jay Kesler, and Grace Olson are heroes of the Christian faith, and their stories are told, retold, and celebrated by students, faculty, and staff as a way of reminding Taylor of its distinction.

Reflecting on my four years at Taylor, I can see now how intentional Taylor's leaders are about culture. Footwashing ceremonies, the names on buildings, the celebrations, the community covenant, and dorm traditions all served to reinforce and propel the values of the institution.

Mission True Culture

Mission True organizations don't underestimate culture. More than anything else, culture predicts the attitudes and actions of their staff. They realize:

1. *Small things matter:* Minor practices go a long way in setting the organization's tone. For example, whether you step foot inside a Chick-Fil-A in Denver or Dallas or Des Moines, the staff will respond to customers with the now famous "My pleasure." This simple act is just one of the many ways that Chick-Fil-A builds a culture of hospitality.

2. *Consistency counts:* Organizations like IJM recognize that fireworks and glossy brochures don't make a culture; rather, it is a daily commitment to repeatable practices. It's in the routine. No matter how busy, all employees recognize that 11 a.m. is sacred—and it's this consistency (and, even more important, faithfulness to God) that has enabled IJM's mission to flourish.

3. *Exemplars should be celebrated:* When staff members exhibit organizational values, be sure to call it out. The surest way to have others embrace your full mission is through positive reinforcement. At each of our staff meetings, staff members nominate their colleagues when they see them living out organizational culture.

4. *Embed spiritual disciplines:* They find ways to build prayer, Scripture, communion, and devotions into their normal work rhythms.

Great organizations get culture. It's been said we are *creatures of habit*. Organizations are *creatures of shared habits*. A lack of habits or bad habits will create the space for drift to occur. Cultivating a purposeful and healthy culture, reinforced by good habits, will carry forward your values and be another safeguard for your mission.

One of the most critical elements of Mission True culture is the way it's spoken about.

14

The Language of the Chameleon Club

Mission True organizations boldly
proclaim their core tenets to
protect themselves from drift

"Language is the apparel in which your thoughts
parade before the public."

—George Crane

A large international nonprofit houses all their marketing materials in a giant storeroom. In towering stacks of boxes, staff members can find all their organizational flyers and letterhead. But they have to choose carefully. Because two iterations of each core piece exist—one for a "churchy" audience and one for a "non-churchy" audience.

Quotes from pastors, Bible verses, and stories of spiritual life change dot the pages of the churchy annual report. It reads like a compelling account of a vibrant faith-based organization.

A quick stroll through the non-churchy edition, however, reveals a whole different organization. Stripped of any spiritual language, this version features quotes and endorsements from leading academics, researchers, and corporate foundations.

The organization has two faces. It reads and feels like two entirely different organizations. And it creates opportunities for confusion.

When the secular version of a letter was inadvertently sent to a key Christian supporter, it caused the organization significant reputational harm. Shortly after the letter was received, executives began reevaluating whether this practice was the right long-term strategy.

Chameleon Club

Early on in my (Peter's) career, I frequented alumni gatherings with my Harvard friends. While there, I skirted around HOPE International's Christian identity like dieters avoid ice cream parlors. Deflecting and sterilizing, I constantly tried to validate HOPE independent of our Christian values.

"HOPE is working to eradicate extreme poverty."

"We practice microfinance in some of the toughest places in the world, like Burundi and Congo."

And sometimes, if I sensed the person might be open to our Christ-centered identity, I'd add, "HOPE is a faith-based organization."

Realizing our core identity would not resonate with every audience and wanting to avoid appearing overzealous, I did no better than the organization with two editions of their annual report. With my church friends, I led with HOPE's Christian identity. With my Harvard friends, I conveniently forgot to mention it.

A card-carrying member of the chameleon club, I've learned how easy it is to blend in with my surroundings. Sometimes it is done with the organization's best interests in mind, but other times it's because I want to be liked. Or seen as relevant. Or I don't want to offend. Or because I'm embarrassed.

But the words of Jesus challenge the chameleon approach: "And I tell you, everyone who acknowledges me before men, the Son of

Man also will acknowledge before the angels of God, but the one who denies me before men will be denied before the angels of God."[1] Without mincing words, it's clear how much our language matters.

Building a Brand

The building industry has been hammered in recent years. However, in the midst of the recession, *Builder Magazine* held the 9th Annual Hearthstone Builder Humanitarian Awards dinner at the Hard Rock Café in Universal Studios. The gala event honored homebuilders who were focused on giving back to their communities and to the world.

Since Jeff Rutt, founder of HOPE International, was one of the award winners, we were able to do a session on our microfinance model for the builder community. In front of a packed room in the Peabody Hotel in Orlando, we shared Jeff's story—how he founded HOPE as a ministry of a local church in Lancaster, Pennsylvania, eager to provide a hand up and not a handout, and how we continue to share Christ as we help empower families to work their way out of poverty.

After the presentation, two staff members from another faith-based organization waited until everyone had left to approach me.

"I can't believe you just said that stuff!" one shared. "This was a secular audience and you spoke about Christ."

He went on, "Ten years ago, we might have mentioned God, but we just can't do that anymore in today's polarized world."

His last question hit me, "Weren't you worried about what people might think?"

Yes, I was worried. Just a year before, I probably would have found a creative way to water down our identity. In other situations, I had not been so bold in sharing our full mission. But I had realized that seemingly minor decisions about how to communicate are either a prevention tool against Mission Drift—or another small step away.

Consistency

Especially in today's hyper-connected world, it just isn't a winning strategy to have two differing messages. It's only a matter of time until a YouTube video or tweet pops the bubble of independence. Consistency is the only way.

Additionally, people value candor. It erodes trust to speak out of two sides of your mouth, communicating one message here and a different message there.

This is not to say you don't ever contextualize your message for your audience. We should design brochures aimed at children and create events suited for pastors. And we should of course avoid using jargon that only Christians can understand. But it's a dangerous practice when it sounds like you're describing two completely different organizations. Honesty trumps pageantry every time.

Accountability

Clear language reinforces identity and also leads to accountability.

A few years ago, my friend Henry made the decision to sell his beach house and give all the proceeds to ministries. After concluding as a family that this was what God wanted them to do, he declared it publicly at an event in North Carolina.

But after listing the house, they had second thoughts. Should they really sell the home and give it all away? However, Henry described how making the public commitment provided an extra push to keep his word.

Being clear with your plans and identity enables people to keep you on mission.

If you regularly talk about who you are, you invite scrutiny and accountability. Publicly proclaiming who you are strengthens your identity and empowers people to point out inconsistencies.

The Language of Water Street

Since 1905, Water Street Ministries has been serving the vulnerable in Lancaster County, Pennsylvania. Known for their provision of food and shelter for the homeless, they also provide healthcare, job training, leadership development of urban youth, early childhood education, and addiction recovery. Their mission statement has remained constant since 1917: "To advance the kingdom of God through the gospel of Jesus Christ, and to do missionary, relief and rescue work of all kinds."

They are an inspiring example of holding on to past identity while looking to the future. But what made the greatest impression during our visits to their facilities was the way they told their story.

No matter what we asked them, they kept returning to Scripture. Appropriately tying their interventions and programs into the biblical narrative, they clearly saw Scripture as the lens from which to minister to those in need.

When talking about their definition of poverty, Steve Brubaker, chief vision officer, shared how they ensure they aren't just "solving problems" while ignoring the importance of real relationships. He gave the example of the interaction Jesus had with a disabled man at the Pool of Bethesda.[2] He described how the unseen tragedy in the story wasn't the man's disability; it was that in thirty-eight years he hadn't cultivated a relationship sufficient to aid him entering the pool. Alone and isolated, he needed more than just physical healing.

In discussing what programs they focus on and when to implement new programs, Steve referenced the story of Lazarus and how "Jesus only did what the Father wanted Him to do." Steve described how, despite the pleas of Lazarus's sisters, Jesus actually waited two whole days before traveling to Bethany.[3] Everything Jesus did was with deliberateness and with His Father's leading. In a similar way, at Water Street Steve didn't want to "jump at the problem" without a more complete understanding of whether it was God's leading and timing.

"A weakened commitment to Scripture, more than any other factor, has facilitated historical drift," wrote Dr. Arnold Cook in *Historical Drift*. He continued, "It renders us vulnerable to the subtle accommodation to culture."[4] It was clear Water Street understood the centrality of Scripture and told their story in the broader context of God's work.

As an organization, they were following the call in Deuteronomy:

These commandments that I give you today are to be on your hearts. Impress them on your children. Talk about them when you sit at home and when you walk along the road, when you lie down and when you get up. Tie them as symbols on your hands and bind them on your foreheads. Write them on the doorframes of your houses and on your gates.[5]

Today social and cognitive scientists recognize the significance of what the ancient Israelites practiced: that what we say changes how we think and remember.

For example, individuals in a survey were asked to watch clips of car accidents. Afterward, one group was asked "How fast were the cars going when they smashed into each other?"

The other group had the same question with one modification: "smash" was not used, but "hit," a more impartial word.

Those who heard "smashed" believed the cars collided at a greater velocity than those with "hit." Later, they also more often (mistakenly) believed glass was shattered because of the accident.[6]

Though the differences were slight, what was said framed what they thought about the accident. Whether or not intended, our words shape our beliefs. What we say has direct influence on the future of our organizations.

Language Anchors

A group of British students founded InterVarsity at the University of Cambridge in 1877. These bold students prayed, studied the Bible, and shared their faith with their classmates, despite the occasional disapproval of university officials. More than 130 years later, Inter-Varsity stands Mission True.

InterVarsity now serves students on over 575 campuses, their leaders' hearts beating to the same cadence as those who founded Inter-Varsity. But like the first InterVarsity groups, they face increasing pressures on campuses across the country.

InterVarsity president Alec Hill understands that their language will impact whether they remain Mission True for the next 130 years. They have core documents all staff members sign clearly articulating their doctrine, purpose, vision, and core values.

But even more important is the way these documents are incorporated when they recruit trustees, staff, and volunteers. A common language reinforces their identity and helps create parameters around who wants to opt in and become part of this community.

At every national conference, InterVarsity leaders go through one of their four core documents and incorporate it into the language they use. Alec knows the importance of language and how it creates a common culture.

Mission True Language

Mission True organizations recognize that it is not just what they do, and not just how they do it, but how they talk about it that matters. Mission True organizations:

1. *Proclaim their full mission to create accountability:* By publicly declaring their mission, they invite others to provide feedback. It empowers people to call them out when they are drifting.
2. *Deploy language anchors:* Weaving Scripture or their core mission tenets into their everyday language provides signposts to ground them toward making decisions based on their mission's objectives.
3. *Build credibility through consistency:* Customers and donors easily discredit organizations if they see inconsistency in messaging. By being open and straightforward, they position themselves as an organization, ministry, or institution that can be trusted.

Language might seem trivial, but the words we use shape our organizations. Language is one of the last things we might think of as a quality of Mission True organizations, but we found it is. We also found Mission True organizations recognize their role and the importance of partnering with God's favorite institution.

15

SAVE THE CHURCH

Mission True organizations recognize
that the local church is the
anchor to a thriving mission

Drift. The very word conjures images of a boat blown by the wind and led by the currents. Lacking a clear destination. Floating aimlessly.

You don't have to be an expert sailor to realize that there is an easy way to prevent your boat from drifting: Throw an anchor overboard.

When I (Peter) was in middle school, my brother and I would carry an old boat on our heads to the Concord River. We'd cast off. I'd do the rowing, Jon the fishing. The boat leaked, which only added to the adventure.

An old cinder block and some rope served as our anchor. Nothing fancy, but it worked. Anchors are perhaps the most ancient of nautical inventions. Cinder blocks, old tires, or welded iron—they all do the trick.

For organizations who desire to protect against Mission Drift, one of the most powerful anchors is the local church.

National Revival to Global Missions

"We were birthed in a church, Park Street Church in Boston," said Stephan Bauman, president and CEO of World Relief.[1]

Park Street Church in historic downtown Boston is home to many "firsts," including introducing Billy Graham to the revival ministry. Graham became a lifelong friend to Park Street Church's pastor, Dr. Harold Ockenga.

Graham said that "nobody outside of my family influenced me more than [Ockenga] did. I never made a major decision without first calling and asking his advice and counsel."[2]

Today Graham and Ockenga are credited as being the bricklayers of a revival toward Christian orthodoxy that swept across the nation.

But Park Street's pastor was concerned with more than his own congregation and those across the country. He was convicted "that missions make the church" and "that the local church is the key to world missions."[3]

He cared deeply for the needy. And he understood God's heart for the vulnerable.

As the president of the National Association of Evangelicals (NAE), Ockenga oversaw the creation of the War Relief Commission, which started partnering with local churches in Eastern Europe following the devastation of World War II.[4]

Today it's known as World Relief, a global relief and development agency serving over four million people through 2,500 staff members and 60,000 volunteers[5] in over 20 countries.[6] World Relief's birthplace was symbolic of its mission to partner with the church, a mission that is still at the heartbeat of the organization today.

"Everything we do is through the local church," shared Bauman.[7]

Relational Drift

For centuries, the local church was the centerpiece of outreach and service. The rapid creation of separate parachurch organizations is a relatively recent phenomenon.

Para, parachurch's prefix, is Greek for "alongside" or "beside."

The purpose of the parachurch organization is to come alongside, to support, the local church.

Following World War II, a concerted effort to respond on a massive scale to the devastation of Europe and Asia began. Newspapers carried images of suffering in Europe and Asia to the doorsteps of many Americans, prompting a compassionate response. A few years later television opened eyes to the world's needs.

The result was the rapid increase of Christian relief and development organizations motivated by faith, but largely disconnected from the local church. Over time, many of these organizations, like Christian Children's Fund, received increased funding from a variety of supporters.

No longer were partnerships with churches necessary. In fact, they sometimes stifled organizational growth. Parachurch ministries and outreach organizations pursued independence.

More significantly, a separation developed between the "works" of justice and the "message" of salvation. Slowly, the church was given the responsibility to share the Good News verbally while the work of physical restoration went to nonprofits.

David Bronkema describes the implications of this period: "In effect, the theological rubber band that held the two elements [of the Good News and good deeds] . . . had snapped."[8] But not all organizations walked away from the local church. Mission True organizations know the importance of collaboration with local congregations.

One of these organizations is World Relief. Today they actively work to connect churches around the world. Every outreach program has to have a clear plan of action grounded in local church partnership. They recruit through local churches and actively seek to strengthen church networks.

World Relief understood from the beginning that the building up of the church is the anchor to the mission.

The Bride or Bridezilla?

Working in close collaboration with like-minded local churches is perhaps the easiest way to stay on mission. But from our experience, it's also among the most complicated.

Several years ago, while working in Rwanda with World Relief, I (Peter) gathered with staff and clients in a rural church to disburse small loans to assist entrepreneurs to start or to expand their businesses. It was a time of celebration. Each client shared a business plan and dreams for the future.

We later learned something alarming: Right after the staff members left, the local pastor called a special meeting with all the clients—a conveniently timed Bible lesson on tithing.

He began his talk describing how the Bible required each member to tithe 10 percent. He then preached that tithing was required on any funds they received.

Since they had all just accepted a small loan to invest in their businesses, he required each member to give him (for the church, of course) 10 percent of the total loan amount. It would be like your pastor showing up after you just took a $100,000 mortgage for your home and required you to "tithe" $10,000.

Members tried to share about the difference between productive investment and profit, but to no avail. If they wanted to continue attending the church, they needed to pay up.

The group of entrepreneurs disbanded after this first cycle, and it was not a positive experience for anyone involved.

On another occasion working for a Christian microfinance organization in Rwanda, I received a recommendation letter from a senior denominational leader. Attesting to Sheila's[9] character, volunteer experience, and capacity, the letter was one of the most glowing reports I'd ever reviewed. We hired her.

Less than a year later, we discovered Sheila was stealing from the organization.

It turns out Sheila was also the niece of the denominational leader who provided the reference. Conveniently, this detail was left out during the application process. Even more disheartening, when we discussed the issue with the denominational leader, he threatened us. He made it clear we'd face issues if we dismissed Sheila. Not denying the allegations, he misused his power to protect a family member.

Unfortunately, this is not an isolated case.

"I know the church is described as the Bride of Christ in Scripture, but too often it acts like Bridezilla," Gil Odendaal of World Relief remarked.[10]

Why would organizations desire to tie themselves to the church when it seems it would be so much easier to operate alone?

No Plan B

At a backyard party a few years ago, Laurel, my wife, overheard a teenager's rude comments making fun of our son. Trying to impress his friends, he used inappropriate words and gestures, unaware an adult was within hearing distance. Laurel grabbed our son and broke into tears as she walked away.

Moments later, when I learned what happened, adrenaline shot through my body. The Papa Bear instinct kicked in. Walking over to the child who made the comments, I communicated that his words and actions were unacceptable. I very clearly suggested he not make them again. "It is time for you to go home. Right. Now."

Nothing makes me react more strongly than someone threatening my wife or children.

In Scripture, God talks repeatedly about the church as His bride.[11] We know this bride has plenty of blemishes, yet she is still Christ's bride. You cannot love the Bridegroom yet show disrespect for the bride.

Imagine a friendship with someone who constantly berated the one you most treasure—it just wouldn't be a friendship for very long. In a similar way, might the Bridegroom not take too kindly to us constantly pointing out the flaws and problems and miss the central point—the church is still His beloved and chosen bride?

In God's wisdom, the local church is God's Plan A. There is no Plan B.[12] His work continues through His chosen instrument. With a supernatural origination and divine mandate, the church is Christ's hands and feet bringing the Good News as we love God and our neighbors. The church is Christ in the world; Christ's bride really makes Him present, at this time, in this place, among these people.

While imperfect, the body of Christ is the anchor, "the church of the living God, a pillar and buttress of the truth."[13] You cannot remain Mission True without a rigorous commitment to Christ's body—the church.

We would be wise to examine the practice of our Catholic friends and even some Protestant denominations. Their parachurch ministries fall under the authority and leadership of the church. This arrangement creates structures and accountability many evangelical ministries lack. For example, World Renew, the Christian Reformed denomination's arm for relief reached more than 1.75 million people with life-changing services in 2011.[14]

Some parachurch ministries recognize the joys of partnering with the local church. Caring Partners International, a short-term medical missions organization, understands that the local church is the sustaining force behind their ministry. Their motto is "Partnering with the local church enables us to turn short-term trips into long-term impact."[15]

Without the local church, Caring Partners recognizes that their ministry is temporary. The church is what sustains the work of Christ for the long haul.

In his book *Walking with the Poor*, Bryant Myers writes that René Padilla in a World Vision workshop highlighted the danger of missing the role of the local church in ministry: "The path to secularization is made straight if you lose sight of the local church."[16]

Consider Habitat for Humanity. Millard Fuller founded the organization out of his faith convictions. In a difficult season of life, he "found God" and created Habitat to provide housing for the poor. His first Habitat project was an experiment while he served as a missionary in Congo.[17]

During his final days, Fuller shared his greatest fear—that his organization would forget its Christian identity. And he noted that Habitat's growth and success were perhaps its biggest downfall.

Millard implored his fellow Baptists to fight for his organization's core:

> I have a deep concern that Habitat for Humanity remain firmly a Christian ministry. From the beginning, I have seen Habitat as a new frontier in Christian missions—a creative and new way to proclaim the gospel. . . . My greatest concern for Habitat for Humanity is going secular.[18]

Without the church serving as an anchor at Habitat, Fuller recognized Habitat would drift.

The church has lasted for over 2,000 years and is a direct link to the teachings of Jesus. Despite humanity's best efforts to crush it, it remains. In his book *Bad Religion: How We Became a Nation of Heretics,* Ross Douthat summarizes,

> You couldn't spend your whole life in Campus Crusade for Christ, or raise your daughter as a Promise Keeper, or count on groups like the Moral Majority or the Christian Coalition to sustain your belief system beyond the next election cycle. For that kind of staying power you needed a confessional tradition, a church, an institution capable of outlasting its charismatic founders.[19]

Wisdom lies in anchoring ourselves to the church as the church is anchored to Christ. Across time and culture and trends, the church remains.

We Can't Do It Alone

The global church needs each member, a lesson enthusiastic North American mission trip participants sometimes need to hear. We all have something to give, and we all have something to receive. For example, I have learned so much about prayer through my brothers and sisters in Rwanda and the Philippines. In the Dominican Republic, the church members have taught me about experiencing joy in Christ as I've never experienced it before. No one person or organization has all the answers. As Paul said, "Just as a body, though one, has many parts, but all its many parts form one body, so it is with Christ."[20]

Though this applies to individuals, it also covers institutions. We are part of a much larger family and independence just isn't an option.

Very rarely do we get a glimpse of Jesus' prayer life. Though we know He frequently sought solitude to spend time with His Father, few passages reveal the prayers. That is what makes Jesus' prayer in John 17 a fascinating glimpse of Christ's heart.

Jesus lays out His intention for the body of Christ:

> My prayer is not for them alone. I pray also for those who will believe in me through their message, that all of them may be one, Father, just

as you are in me and I am in you. May they also be in us so that the
world may believe that you have sent me. I have given them the glory
that you gave me, that they may be one as we are one—I in them and
you in me—so that they may be brought to complete unity. Then the
world will know that you sent me and have loved them even as you
have loved me.[21]

Unity is the central characteristic of the body of Christ. And it's
this unity, Christ says, that will compel others to pay attention to the
message of grace.

In essence, we have the opportunity to fulfill Christ's prayer when
we partner with the local church in a spirit of friendship and mutual
dependence.

The World's Largest Social Network

While operating in a closed country context, an organization had a
fantastic problem—people were coming to Christ.

In fact, one survey revealed that 59 percent of families served heard
about Christ *for the very first time* from staff members serving their
community. Many individuals made a profession of faith and desired
to gather together to "do church." Eager to help and thrilled at the
impact, staff members began home churches.

These independent churches began growing and taking on church-
planting responsibilities. But it didn't take long for the problems to start.
Questions of belief and practice came flooding in. With little training
and no support, the staff members were unsure how to handle these
challenges. They didn't have the foundation to disciple others into mature, growing Christ-followers. These challenges impacted their service.

Their expertise was in community development, and they struggled
to understand how to navigate key issues related to growing home
churches. Clearly, they needed help.

After several years of frustration, the group changed the approach
and partnered with a local group of churches eager to expand to these
communities. It was a symbiotic relationship—the local church had a
new outreach tool, and the ministry was able to focus on its programs.
Truly a win/win partnership.

The church as church, and the parachurch at her side.

No entity is more expansive than the local church. Pastor and author of *The Purpose Driven Life,* Rick Warren illustrates this principle by laying out three maps of the Western Province of Rwanda. In the first map, three small dots mark the locations of hospitals. The second map identifies the eighteen health clinics that serve 700,000 people. The third map identifies the churches—826 dots cover the map. This visual powerfully conveys that the church has a far greater scope and scale than virtually any other social entity in the region.[22]

Beyond these practical benefits, the underlying reason for partnership is that it binds organizations to their mission. The church grounds all good works in the grander vision of humanity's fall and God's redemption. It's not easy, but for most organizations desiring to stay Mission True, the question with local church partnerships should be "How do we partner?" not "Should we partner?"

Building the Church

When working with World Relief and living in Rwanda, I (Peter) visited a rural church. Made of bricks, its structure was quite simple. But it was extraordinary because Rwandan villagers had built it with their own hands.

World Relief had been serving in the community for several years, assisting with microenterprise development and child survival services.

As the community grew stronger, the local members identified the need for a central place of worship. Pooling their savings from their increased business profits, they dedicated the money to building the church.

Together, they laid its foundation. Together, they built its structure, brick by brick.

When I met with the community members, they said to me, "See what the Lord has accomplished through us." And it wasn't just a building; they were even prouder of the way they provided for widows and orphans.

World Relief, born out of the church, was assisting in the birthing of this and many other churches around the world. And in the process, they throw another anchor overboard to grasp an even firmer hold of their mission.

Mission True and the Church

If you believe the church is a vital component of your mission, there are a few simple, yet effective ways to minimize confusion and work more effectively together. Mission True organizations:

1. *Invest relationally:* Relationships are essential, but they take time. Investing in the local church leadership and building true friendships creates a foundation for collaboration.
2. *Over-communicate:* It's insufficient to have preliminary conversations and a memorandum of understanding. Regularly communicate progress and key metrics, and listen to the church's feedback. One pastor in a rural part of Rwanda told me about my lackluster communication and stated, "We want to support you, but we need to know what you're doing!"
3. *Are generous:* They use their platforms and ministries to invite participants to attend local church events. If we're truly all on the same team, we must actively promote others.
4. *Communicate with clarity:* There is always the possibility of "he said/she said" with partnerships of any sort. Especially cross-culturally, spending additional time clarifying roles, responsibilities, and commitments in writing grounds the partnership.
5. *Worship and pray communally:* Fellowship through worshiping and praying together strengthens connection and reminds us of our common position as men and women united in Christ.
6. *Are learners:* They seek unfiltered perspectives from global church partners and realize how much each group has to learn from the other.

As simple as these suggestions are, they create a more meaningful and impactful partnership.

Church As Anchor

My brother and I used a cinder block as an anchor. Its mass served to steady our boat. Modern anchors often not only provide a mass to balance a boat; they also stabilize it by gripping the seafloor.

When the anchor is first released, it bounces along the ocean floor before snagging the seabed. For a moment, the ship can sway—until the anchor grips the floor, stopping its drift. The church can help anchor us to our mission and identity. And it can help us stay Mission True.

CONCLUSION

As I (Peter) was packing up and getting ready to leave Rwanda to return to graduate school, my pastor warned, "People who go to schools like Harvard end up walking away from their faith. Please don't let it happen to you."

When I arrived in Cambridge, I braced myself for the secular assault on my faith. But what I found surprised me. Despite Harvard's steady institutional drift since its founding, there is simply no doubt that God is still changing hearts in the halls once officially devoted to *Christo et Ecclesiae*, Christ and the Church.

Once in Cambridge, I received an invitation to a barbecue at Jeff Barneson's home. Jeff led InterVarsity Christian Fellowship on the campus, and I was amazed at how many people were there. Even before classes started, I realized Harvard was full of people eager to live out their faith. I struck up a friendship with Jimmy, and we decided to meet regularly to pray for the school and our classmates.

But an even greater surprise was that throughout my graduate school experience, there was surprising openness to issues of faith. My classmates were incredibly intelligent, driven, and compassionate. They were not bombastic, but rather open to thoughtful conversation. We all had questions and were there to thoughtfully discuss answers.

When Billy Graham asked Harvard's former president Derek Bok, "What is the biggest problem among today's students?" Bok replied,

"Emptiness."[1] To fill this emptiness, many students are asking real questions about life. And none of us had the intellectual audacity to claim we had figured it all out.

In its early years, Harvard overtly encouraged students to explore the relevance of Scripture and faith in all areas of life. While not explicit today, there still is honest exploration. And despite the changed mission, people are coming to Christ at Harvard.

While in Cambridge, I read a book called *Finding God at Harvard*, and I realized my experience was not an anomaly. While some walked away from their faith, many others found new faith in Christ while studying.[2]

Harvard's motto, *Veritas*, "was just another, shorthand way of recognizing Jesus Christ, who was seen as the ultimate Truth."[3] Throughout the university, lives are being transformed as the God of Truth continues to reveal the divine in the midst of honest pursuit.

However, as much as we see God still at work at Harvard, we can't help but wonder what would have happened if Harvard had remained true to its original purpose.

What if this institution had figured out how to rigorously pursue academic excellence without giving up the quest for Truth?

What if leaders had learned to stimulate innovation but not at the cost of losing their core identity?

What if they trained men and women for global engagement yet also encouraged leaders to devote themselves fully to the living God?

What if it had remained Mission True?

Harvard, ChildFund, and the Y slowly drifted, and the world will never know what would have happened if they continued to be Mission True.

Today, too many boards, staff, and leaders are silently choosing to follow this well-worn path of Mission Drift.

Monitoring inputs and outputs, they forget to measure what matters most—their ability to implement their full mission. They hire for technical competency alone. Soft-pedaling their Christian identity, they do not defend their mission. Growth becomes their primary definition of success.

However, in researching this book, we discovered there is another option chosen by courageous Mission True leaders. The more we learned their stories, the more we were encouraged. From their founding, these leaders have stood unwaveringly upon the Truth of the Gospel. In all areas, they have demonstrated intentionality and clarity in retaining Christian distinctiveness. They are committed to Christ, first and foremost.

Today, you have the privilege of choosing which path your organization, church, and ministry will take. Will you follow the path toward Mission Drift or will you have the intentionality, courage, and resolve to follow a path of faithfulness?

Imagine the potential impact of a generation choosing to remain Mission True.

Review Questions

Chapter 1—The Unspoken Crisis

- What decisions could draw you away from your core purpose and identity?
- Have you ever experienced a time when a partner or donor has asked you to "tone down" your faith or mission?
- Do you believe that Mission Drift is a real possibility for every organization?

Chapter 2—The Tale of Two Presbyterian Ministers

- What is your organization's source of heat? Is there passion around the cause?
- Are there any small decisions being made for your organization that you believe could lead to Mission Drift?
- In its simplest form, what comprises a Mission True organization?
- How do you know if growth and adaptation are enhancing your mission or leading you off course?
- Have you seen examples of Mission Drift? How did you know it was happening?

Chapter 3—Functional Atheism

- Have you witnessed the "ugly secret" that Kristof discusses?
- Do you believe the consequences of the "ugly secret" are avoidable?
- If Christ-centered faith is part of your mission, has it stayed at the forefront of your organization's operations and service?
- Do you believe that the Gospel is an essential part of your ministry?
- Where might your organization be at most risk of secularization?
- Do the people in your organization fully support the spiritual integration of faith into service?

Chapter 4—Death by Minnows

- Has your organization ever faced a situation similar to the one faced by Dr. Mohler and Southern Seminary? What were the results?
- Is your organization characterized by high or low intentionality? High or low clarity?
- Is there anything underlying in your organization that is being avoided because it might hurt?
- Are you ready and willing to address the tough issues in order to remain Mission True?

Chapter 5—The Secret Recipe to Quaker Oats

- Do you already have safeguards in place to avoid drifting from your mission?
- What safeguards and barriers can you establish to ensure that drift does not occur in the future, like Henry Crowell?
- Is your board making decisions that do not reflect the original mission?
- What steps have you as a board member, or the other board members of your organization, taken to safeguard the mission?

Chapter 6—You Know Why You Exist

- Does your organization have a strong sense of core purpose and identity?

- Have you or your organization faced challenging moments like InterVarsity at Vanderbilt? How did you react?

- What have you seen successfully change in your organization while it has remained Mission True?

- Has your organization, or you, lost its "saltiness" in any way?

- Can you brainstorm any ideas to regain your distinct "salty" flavor as an organization? How about ways to sustain and grow it?

- What are your "immutables"?

Chapter 7—Guardians of the Mission

- Have you ever faced disconnect between yourself and a board, like Mary Smith?

- What key decisions has your board made recently to support the mission of your organization?

- Does your board communicate the decisions it makes to employees? Is it transparent?

- How can your board promote accountability within its ranks to avoid situations such as CAI and Greg Mortenson?

- Do you have a process for inviting people onto your board? Are you able to clearly list it? Do results show that it has been effective historically?

Chapter 8—True Leadership

- Do you believe in the Machiavellian adage, "the ends justify the means"? Why or why not?

- Have you believed you were immune to spiritual and moral dangers or do you believe "It could happen to me"?

- What spiritual disciplines do you and your leadership engage in to remain grounded in Christ?
- Does your organization or company have an appropriate succession plan to recruit Mission True talent?

Chapter 9—Impressive Credentials Are Not Enough

- What hiring practices does your organization/company utilize?
- What values are you, your employees, and fellow colleagues setting for the next generation of workers entering the workforce, and your company?
- Does your organization hire based on job skills or also for mission fit? How?
- Does your recruitment strategy correspond to the reason you exist and what you hope to accomplish?
- Based on the mission of your organization, do you have a statement of faith for leaders and staff?
- What else have you learned about recruiting and retaining staff who fully live out your mission?

Chapter 10—Follow the Money

- Are those who fund your mission in line with the full mission of your organization?
- Do you pay attention to funders like Greg, who humbly spoke the truth in love about something "little" like the message of a video?
- Do your donors take the role of safeguarding the mission seriously?
- What are things you can do to safeguard your organization's mission from the potential influence of donors who do not fully share your mission?
- Are you as an individual actively seeking to support organizations that fall in line with your beliefs? Are you doing your homework before giving?

- Are you questioning inconsistency or any seeds of Mission Drift in the organizations you support (by speaking the truth in love and praying about it beforehand)?

- Have you taken steps to ensure your funds will be given according to your wishes after you're gone? If not, take a first step today and create a one-page summary of your values and philanthropic priorities.

- What are some practical ways you can involve your family with giving and teach them about thoughtful philanthropy?

Chapter 11—Measuring What Matters

- What key performance indicators drive your organization? Is your organization exclusively focused on donations raised and the number of people served? Are you being successful in areas that ultimately don't matter to your organization's success?

- What is not measured slowly becomes irrelevant. What are areas you could measure that relate more directly to your mission?

- What are your thoughts on Youth For Christ's decision to significantly alter what they measure?

- If you already have ways to measure success (beyond fundraising or number of people served), do they help you keep the vision of your organization always before you?

- Has there ever been a time when you have taken the glory because of your own efforts? If so, what have you done to remember it's not about you?

Chapter 12—Etched in Excellence

- Have you ever considered the fact that substandard work could undermine the message of your mission?

- Is your organization known for excellence? How do you know?

- Are you willing to start from scratch if your work falls short?

- What steps can you begin to implement to ensure the highest level of quality?

Chapter 13—Culture Eats Strategy for Breakfast

- What little things are you implementing into your culture that promote your organization's values?
- What daily or weekly rituals are you as a leader implementing to develop a healthy culture? (For example, all IJM employees turn everything off, stop work, and pray at 11 a.m. each day.)
- What is the "everyday nature" of your organization (like Southwest's customer service)? How is this being conveyed not only to your employees, but also to your donors?
- As a leader, what are you doing to lead everyone with purpose and intentionality?
- Are there any bad habits or aspects of your culture that need to be tossed?

Chapter 14—The Language of the Chameleon Club

- Does your organization have two faces?
- Trust is eroded when you speak two different messages. Have you ever been a "card-carrying member of the chameleon club"?
- Being candid and honest about the mission of your organization not only strengthens your identity but invites _____?
- Is your organization following what Jesus commands us in Deuteronomy 6:6–9 and Luke 12:8–9?
- In what ways is your language consistent or inconsistent with your mission?

Chapter 15—Save the Church

- We must remember that the local church is God's Plan A. Are you currently partnered with a local church? If so, how?

- If you are currently partnering with the bride of Christ, are you using clarity and overcommunicating?
- The church binds organizations to the grander vision of man's fall and God's redemption. Read 1 Corinthians 12:12–31. How can you seek to embody this with your partnerships?

Acknowledgments

A page of acknowledgments at the end of this book is woefully inadequate to properly thank the team of friends who made this book happen. With no false humility do we acknowledge this book was a joint effort of our remarkable friends and colleagues.

Alli and Laurel, your insights and conversations along the way clarified our thinking and strengthened our resolve. Thank you for encouraging us to pursue work we love. We clearly married up.

We would like to acknowledge the important roles our families have played in supporting us through this writing process. I (Chris) would like to thank my parents and brothers, Matthew and Jonathan, for their ongoing enthusiasm about my work. I (Peter) would like to thank the entire Greer and Steinweg families for their involvement, editing, and overwhelming support of these projects.

Anna Haggard, your hard work and brilliant writing sharpened our arguments. We are thankful you decided to intern with HOPE three years ago and grateful you haven't stopped writing with us since.

Stephanie Walker, from Lancaster to Ukraine, your astute research savvy helped us capture key details of these stories. This book has depth it simply wouldn't have had without you.

Andrew Wolgemuth, we could not possibly ask for any more support or thoughtful insights from our agent. Thank you for being the first person to see the potential of this book.

Andy McGuire, more than just an acquisitions editor, you are a friend who believed in this book. Thank you for walking with us throughout the process.

Ellen Chalifoux, Carra Carr, Brett Benson, Erin Hollister, and the Bethany team, once again, you impressed us with your professionalism and a commitment to excellence. You excel at what you do.

Bailie Porter, Sean Williams, and Annie Eggleston—we couldn't have gotten to the finish line without your amazing research and fact checking.   ·

To all the people and organizations who graciously allowed us to probe and explore your mission, thank you. It is your stories we celebrate and your example we want to follow. Special thanks to Stephan Bauman, Alec Hill, Dan Wolgemuth, Candy Sparks, Chuck Buck, Mark Taylor, Bruce Konold, Kim Phipps, Marty Caldwell, Lisa Espineli Chinn, Steve Haas, Gil Odendaal, Cyprien Nkiriyumwami, Steve Brubaker, Merv Auchtung, Bryant Myers, Jonathan Merritt, Scott Sabin, John Warton, Durwood Snead, Chris Crane, Hunter Baker, P. Lowell Haines, Stephanie Summers, Henry Kaestner, Gideon Strauss, Drew Cleveland, Stanley Carlson-Thies, Steve James, Tim Skrivan, Dr. Eugene Habecker, Dave Shoemaker and the C12 Group, and Dr. Ben Sells.

To our panel of experts who helped us identify the Mission True organizations, thank you for being right on target in pointing us to some remarkable organizations. Steve Perry, Jimmy Lee, Al Mueller, Chad Hayward, Rudy Carrasco, Keith Davy, Amy Sherman, Greg Lafferty, Ron Webb, Brian Fikkert, Bob Andringa, Steve Beers, Dr. Bill Ringenberg, Josh Kwan, Fred Smith, John Lewis, Steven Laird, Owen Strachan, and Aimee Watkins.

Special thanks to Dave Larson, David Bronkema, Benj Petroelje, and Terry Looper, who each donated many hours to sharpening our ideas.

To our friends who read early drafts of the book and pushed us to sharpen our arguments and polish our writing, we are grateful. Your fingerprints are all over this book and it is a better final product because of you. Don and Patty Wolf, Jeff Haanen, Joanna Meyer, John Kelly, J. R. Briggs, Steve and Jeanie Laird, Tim Hoiland, Aaron Leclaire, Amy Bordoni, Marshall Birkey, Bob Quinn, Bonnie and Steve Wurzbacher, Bryan Dunagan, Cathi Linch, Chad Stewart, Chris and

Sarah Chancey, Chris Marlink, Cliff Benson, Cronan Connell, Dalton Sirmans, Dan MacClellan, Dave Clouse, Dave Runyon, Eric Thurman, Greg and Helene Watts, Hunter Beaumont, Isaac Ezell, Jeremy Carver, Jesse and Krista Casler, John Weiser, Katie Nienow, Lance Wood, Mark Conklin, Mark Nottingham, Marlin Horst, Matthew Lee Anderson, Michael Chiarelli, Paul Penley, Phil Smith, Ruckshan Fernando, Ryan McMonagle, Sarah Robinson, Scott Todd, Steve Mayer, Tiger Dawson, Tim Sandlund, Todd Ream, Tom McMurry, Tyler Green, Cole Costanzo, Phil Clemens, Scott Sonju, Alan and Katherine Barnhart, Billy Nolan, Bob and Leslie Doll, Bob Rowling, Brad Lomenick, Bryson Volgetanz, Cary Paine, Daryl Heald, David Wills, David Weekley, Dennis Hollinger, Glen Lucke, Greg Campbell, Jeff Shinabarger, Jeremie Kubichek, Jim Deitch, Joel Dobberpuhl, John Patchell, John T. Lewis, Jon Tyson, Kelly Monroe Kullberg, Kevin Hunt, Kelly Phipps, Kurt Keilhacker, Matt Bennett, Nancy Duncan, Rusty Walter, Timothy Ogden, Todd Harper, and Todd Hendricks.

To the Board of HOPE International, thank you for your support of this project and graciously providing the space to write Mission Drift. More important, thank you for faithfully being the guardians of the HOPE International mission.

To our HOPE International colleagues, thank you for your passion for the Gospel and for keeping HOPE a Mission True organization. On we go!

To our Lord and Savior, your grace changes everything. It is your story of love and redemption we want to share with our words and mirror in our lives.

Soli Deo Gloria.

Proceeds from this book support HOPE International and the Mission True organizations celebrated in this book.

Appendix 1

Board of Directors Prospective Board Member Nomination Form

- A prospective board member must be nominated by an existing board member.
- The nominating board member will fill out a nomination form, which includes a statement making the case for the recommendation of the prospective board member.
- The nominating member must submit a bio, the nominating form, and the recommendation to the board development subcommittee for consideration.
- The board development subcommittee researches candidates and evaluates their fit with the board's needs and mission.
- The subcommittee brings the recommendation to the entire board of directors.
- The board of directors votes on the nomination. (Note: Voting may be done either at a board meeting or via conference call.)

Only at this point does the committee reach out and interview the prospective candidate.

- The board development subcommittee extends an invitation to the prospective board member if the nomination is approved and the interview is successful.

Prospective Board Member Information

Name:	
Mailing Address:	
City/State/Zip:	
Country:	
Work Phone:	
Cell Phone:	
E-Mail:	
If Married, Name of Spouse:	
If Children, Names of Children and Years Born:	
Home Church (Name/Location):	
Profession/Title:	
Employer (Name/ Location):	

Prospective Board Member's Areas of Expertise

AREA OF EXPERTISE		NOTES
Technical Competence/ Strategic Planning	☐	
Discipleship/Outreach	☐	
Finance/Audit	☐	
Fundraising/Donor Relationships	☐	
Governance	☐	
Marketing/Messaging	☐	
Systems/IT	☐	

Other skill sets that the prospective board member has that you feel would be valuable:

Reasons for Recommendation

Describe your relationship with the prospective board member and share a bit about what you know about him/her.

Why do you believe the prospective board member would be a good fit with the board of directors?

On which board subcommittee do you think the prospective board member would be able to most effectively serve and why?

What has been the candidate's commitment to Christian mission?

Appendix 2

Primacy of Proclamation Board Resolution

Resolved: The primary purpose of [insert name of organization] is to [insert purpose]. It is hereby resolved that this primary purpose of proclaiming Jesus Christ cannot be changed unless there are unanimous votes of 100% of all then duly elected members of the [insert organization name] board of directors at face-to-face meetings in three consecutive years. In other words, changing this primary purpose shall take no less than three years to do and there must be at least one face-to-face board meeting in each of three consecutive years with all the then current board members attending each of the three meetings, not just a quorum, at which all board members unanimously vote to change this primary purpose at each of the three meetings.[1]

Appendix 3

Family Giving Charter

It is our intent by this memo to provide guidance to all future generations involved in this foundation or with proceeds from this foundation as to its purpose and mission.

Our appeal to you is not to drift from the ultimate purpose of helping change and redeem lives through the powerful Gospel of Jesus Christ. There are many good causes and good agencies that deserve funding because of their help to the less fortunate, and there are numerous individuals and foundations that support such causes as long as they are secular. There are far fewer who focus their giving toward conservative Christian endeavors.

In our "post-Christian" era these endeavors need all the support they can gain to remain effective and viable in their ministries. Our purpose is to limit and focus our financial support to such specifically Christian endeavors.

We believe strongly in Christian education and its ability to impact lives for Christ during crucial "tipping points" of the lives of young people. Many schools founded with this intent have drifted toward liberalism or completely secular agendas. We attempt to support those who have stayed true to their spiritual heritage like [institutions listed here].

We support and encourage you to support individual missionaries, preferably ones with long and successful track records, as too many new missionaries leave their calling just as they become effective, after three to five years. We prefer to support those on the front lines of bringing the Good News of salvation in Jesus Christ to a lost world. In supporting individual missionaries, one-time gifts can make big differences. Monthly support is most valued, but must be carefully considered, for once started it is very difficult to withdraw.

We often are involved in "support or helping" endeavors, and while these are needed and effective, we want to focus on the front lines, that is, those who are on the foreign mission field. We believe individual missionaries should belong to and be accountable to a larger organization because we all need goals, evaluation, and accountability. For example, agencies such as [ministries listed here] are those in which we have confidence because of their conservative Christian values.

Finally and to repeat, it is our desire that the funds will always be strictly focused on the propagation of the Gospel of Jesus Christ, which changes lives and provides an eternal purpose for living.

Methodology for Mission Drift Research

- Sectors included in research:
  - international social sector
  - domestic social sector
  - educational institutions
  - charitable foundations
  - denominations/church networks
  - businesses
- 5–8 experts in each of the above sectors identified 3–5 organizations within their sphere of influence that they considered *Mission True* exemplars.
- Guidelines for selection included considering the following characteristics:
  - **Stood the test of time:** Organizations have existed for fifty years or more (founded in 1962 or earlier).
  - **Recruited substantial sums of funding:** Organizations have recruited a minimum of $50 million in cumulative funding over their organization's history.
  - **Demonstrated an overtly Gospel-centered mission:** Organizations were established with a clear Christian commitment evidenced in their original documents, mission, and founders.

Notes

Foreword by Andy Crouch

The Scripture quotation at the end of the foreword is from 1 Thessalonians 5:24.

Chapter 1: The Unspoken Crisis

1. Derek Bok, "The President's Report: Harvard University," 1986–87.

2. William C. Ringenberg, *The Christian College* (Grand Rapids, MI: Baker Academic, 2006), 39.

3. "Yale University, About History." Yale University, 2013, www.yale.edu/about/history.html.

4. "Special Edition (Fall 2011) Harvard University at 375 Years: True Confessions," Paideia: Making Excellent Possible (Stony Brook, NY: PAIDEIA, 2011), 2.

5. Ibid., 3.

6. Lawrence Summers, "Convocation of the Divinity School of Harvard University," Harvard University, 2002, www.harvard.edu/president/speeches/summers_2002/convocation.php.

7. Chris Crane, interview by Peter Greer, February 2013.

8. Martin Schlag and Juan Andres Mercado, *Free Markets and the Culture of Common Good* (New York: Springer, 2012), 102.

9. "Fifth Lateran Council," *New Advent: Catholic Encyclopedia*, www.newadvent.org/cathen/09018b.htm.

10. "Pawnbroking," *Encyclopedia Britannica,* www.britannica.com/
EBchecked/topic/447418/pawnbroking.

11. Hugh D. Young and Roger A. Freedman, *University Physics 11th Edition,* "The Second Law of Thermodynamics," July 23, 2003, http://hep.ucsb.
edu/courses/ph23/Chap20Text.pdf.

12. Albert Mohler, "The Cost of Conviction (Part 2)," 2003 Leadership Conference, Sovereign Grace Ministries. www.sovereigngracestore.com/Product/
A2085-03-51B/The_Cost_of_Conviction_(Part_2)_MP3_DOWNLOAD
.aspx.

13. Q Ideas Los Angeles Focus Group Data, conducted in April 2013.

Chapter 2: The Tale of Two Presbyterian Ministers

1. Larry Tise, *A Book About Children: Christian Children's Fund 1938–
1991* (Rapidan, VA: Hartland Publications, 1992), excerpted at http://home
page.isomedia.com/~awin/CCF/Creation.html.

2. Ibid.

3. ChildFund International, "ChildFund History and Story" www.child
fund.org/about_us/mission_and_history/ChildFund_History.aspx.

4. Ken Walker, "Sponsoring a Movement," *Christianity Today,* June 2013,
www.christianitytoday.com/ct/2013/june/sponsoring-movement.html?paging
=off.

5. Randy Frame, "Christian Children's Fund Probed," *Christianity Today,*
November 14, 1994, www.christianitytoday.com/ct/1994/november14/4td071b.
html.

6. William P. Barrett, "The 200 Largest U.S. Charities," *Forbes,* November
30, 2011, www.forbes.com/lists/2011/14/200-largest-us-charities-11_rank.
html.

7. Randy Frame, "Christian Children's Fund Probed."

8. "How Christian Is Christian Children's Fund?" Ministry Watch Donor
Alert, May 2004, www.ministrywatch.com/mw2.1/pdf/MWDA_042704_CCF.
pdf.

9. Abny Santicola, "What's in a Name?" *Fundraising Success,* January 2010, www.fundraisingsuccessmag.com/article/a-lot-found-childfund-
international-to-dispel-misconceptions-better-communicate-the-global-scope
-its-brand-70-year-old-organization-recently-embarked-brand-makeover-
has-invigorated-staff-and-donors-alike-415393/1.

10. Mark Hrywna, "The Name Game," *The NonProfit Times*, June 15, 2009, www.thenonprofittimes.com/article/detail/the-name-game-2376.

11. Kathleen Ja Sook Bergquist, *International Korean Adoption: A Fifty-Year History of Policy and Practice* (New York: Routledge, 2007), 39.

12. "Compassion's History—1950s," *Compassion International*, www.compassion.com/about/history/1950s/.

13. Phil de Haan, "50 Years and Counting: The Impact of the Korean War on the People of the Peninsula," Calvin College, May 2002, .www.calvin.edu/news/2001-02/korea.htm.

14. "Man of Compassion," Advocates Network Compilation DVD, produced by Compassion International.

15. "Financial Integrity," *Compassion International*, www.compassion.com/about/financial.htm.

16. Tami Heim, "More on Leadership from Dr. Wess Stafford," Christian Leadership Alliance, April 3, 2013, http://blog.christianleadershipalliance.org/2013/04/03/more-on-leadership-from-dr-wess-stafford/.

17. *Annual Report 2011–2012*, Compassion International, 2012, www.compassion.com/multimedia/compassion-international-2012-annual-report.pdf.

18. Matthew 7:3–5

19. Joshua 24:15

20. 2 Timothy 4:7

21. 1 Timothy 1:15

Chapter 3: Functional Atheism

1. Nicholas D. Kristof, "Moonshine or the Kids?" *The New York Times*, May 22, 2010, www.nytimes.com/2010/05/23/opinion/23kristof.html?hp.

2. Name and some details changed.

3. Nicholas D. Kristof, "Moonshine or the Kids?"

4. Matthew Parris, "As an Atheist, I Truly Believe Africa Needs God," The Richard Dawkins Foundation, January 7, 2009, http://richarddawkins.net/articles/3502-matthew-parris-as-an-atheist-i-truly-believe-africa-needs-god.

5. Michael Barnett and Janice Gross Stein, "Introduction: The Secularization and Sanctification of Humanitarianism," in Michael Barnett and Janice Gross Stein, editors, *Sacred Aid* (New York: Oxford University Press, 2012), 4.

6. Ibid., 20.

7. Ibid.

8. Bertrand Taithe, "Pyrrhic Victories? French Catholic Missionaries, Modern Expertise, and Secularizing Technologies," in Michael Barnett and Janice Gross Stein, editors, *Sacred Aid* (New York: Oxford University Press, 2012), 181.

9. Kenneth I. Pargament, "Religious Methods of Coping: Resources for the Conservation and Transformation of Significance," in Edward P. Shafranske, editor, *Religion and the Clinical Practice of Psychology* (Washington, D.C.: American Psychological Association, 1996), 232.

10. Jonathan Sacks, "Reversing the Decay of London Undone: Britain's chief rabbi on the moral disintegration since the 1960s and how to rebuild," *The Wall Street Journal,* August 20, 2011, http://online.wsj.com/article/SB1 0001424053111903639404576516252066723110.html.

11. Chris Heath, "The Unbearable Bradness of Being," *Rolling Stone,* Issue 824, October 28, 1999, 72.

12. Rodney Stark, *The Rise of Christianity: How the Obscure, Marginal Jesus Movement Became the Dominant Religious Force in the Western World in a Few Centuries* (New York: HarperCollins, 1997), 73–84.

13. "Charitable Revolution," University of Dayton, February 12, 2013, www.udayton.edu/news/articles/2013/02/beauregard_king_lecture.php.

14. Arthur C. Brooks, "Religious Faith and Charitable Giving," Hoover Institution, October 1, 2003, www.hoover.org/publications/policy-review/article/6577.

15. Barnett and Stein, *Sacred Aid,* cover.

16. John 6:35 ESV

17. Colossians 1:22

18. Tami Heim, "More on Leadership from Dr. Wess Stafford," Christian Leadership Alliance, April 3, 2013, http://blog.christianleadershipalliance.org/2013/04/03/more-on-leadership-from-dr-wess-stafford/.

19. James K. A. Smith, "Naturalizing 'Shalom': Confessions of a Kuyperian Secularist," *Comment* magazine, www.cardus.ca/comment/article/3993/naturalizing-shalom-confessions-of-a-kuyperian-secularist/, June 28, 2013.

20. Dr. Bryant Myers, personal interview with Chris Horst and Peter Greer, February 28, 2013.

21. Email to Peter Greer, June 10, 2013.

22. Matthew Parris, "As an Atheist, I Truly Believe Africa Needs God."

Chapter 4: Death by Minnows

1. Albert Mohler, "The Cost of Conviction (Part 2)," 2003 Leadership Conference, Sovereign Grace Ministries, www.sovereigngracestore.com/Product/A2085-03-51B/The_Cost_of_Conviction_(Part_2)_MP3_DOWNLOAD.aspx.

2. Collin Hansen, "Young, Restless, Reformed," *Christianity Today*, September 22, 2006, www.christianitytoday.com/ct/2006/september/42.32.html?paging=off.

3. Al Mohler, "Don't Just Do Something; Stand There! Southern Seminary and the Abstract of Principles," A Convocation Address Delivered by R. Albert Mohler, Jr., President, The Southern Baptist Theological Seminary, August 31, 1993, in Alumni Memorial Chapel, *Founders Ministries*, www.founders.org/stand.html.

4. Albert Mohler, "The Cost of Conviction (Part 1)," 2003 Leadership Conference, Sovereign Grace Ministries, www.sovereigngracestore.com/Product/A2085-03-51A/The_Cost_of_Conviction(Part_1)_MP3_DOWNLOAD.aspx.

5. Collin Hansen, *Young, Restless, and Reformed* (Wheaton, IL: Crossway, 2008), 72.

6. "About: We Are Serious About the Gospel," The Southern Baptist Theological Seminary, www.sbts.edu/about/.

7. Steve Haas, personal interview with the authors, February 11, 2013.

8. Derek Bok, "The President's Report," 1986–87.

9. Tami Heim, "More on Leadership from Dr. Wess Stafford," Christian Leadership Alliance, April 3, 2013, http://blog.christianleadershipalliance.org/2013/04/03/more-on-leadership-from-dr-wess-stafford/.

10. Gene Habecker, personal interview with Chris Horst, March 13, 2013.

11. Dr. Ben Sells, interview with Chris Horst, March 2013.

12. Lisa Espineli Chinn, interview with Peter Greer, February 2013.

13. Dr. David Bronkema, interview with Chris Horst, October 2012.

14. James 1:2–3 NIV

Chapter 5: The Secret Recipe to Quaker Oats

1. "Quaker History," Quaker Oats, www.quakeroats.com/about-quaker-oats/content/quaker-history.aspx.

2. "Great American Business Leaders of the Twentieth Century—Henry Crowell," Harvard Business School, www.hbs.edu/leadership/database/leaders/henry_p_crowell.html.

3. Richard Ellsworth Day, *Breakfast Table Autocrat* (Whitefish, MT: Kessinger Publishing, 2010), 196.

4. Ibid., 198.

5. Ibid., 209.

6. Ibid., 285.

7. Ibid., 273.

8. Ibid., 274.

9. Ibid.

10. Candy Sparks, email interview with Chris Horst.

11. Waldemar A. Nielsen, *Golden Donors* (New York: Truman Talley Books, 1985), 169.

12. Ibid., 168, 173.

13. Dwight Burlingame, *Philanthropy in America* (Santa Barbara, CA: ABC-CLIO, Inc., 2004), 373.

14. Ibid.

15. "J. Howard Pew," Philanthropy Roundtable, www.philanthropyround table.org/almanac/great_men_and_women/hall_of_fame/j._howard_pew.

16. Billy Graham, *Just As I Am* (New York: HarperCollins, 1999), 286–288.

17. Neela Banerjee, "Accolades, Some Tearful, for a Preacher in His Twilight Years," *The New York Times*, June 1, 2007, www.nytimes.com/2007/06/01/us/01graham.html.

18. Martin Morse Wooster, *The Great Philanthropists and the Problem of "Donor Intent,"* (Capital Research Center, 3rd edition, January 1, 2007), 44.

19. Lucinda Fleeson, "How a Foundation Reinvented Itself," *The Philadelphia Inquirer*, April 27, 1992, http://articles.philly.com/1992-04-27/news/26001700_1_pew-grants-pew-officials-foundation.

20. Ibid.

21. Ibid.

22. "A Matter of Trust," PhilanthropyRoundtable, www.philanthropy roundtable.org/topic/excellence_in_philanthropy/a_matter_of_trust.

23. 1 Corinthians 12:19–20 ESV

Chapter 6: You Know Why You Exist

1. "YMCA Historical Figures: Sir George Williams (1821–1905)," YMCA, www.ymca.int/who-we-are/history/ymca-historical-figures/.

2. John A. Murray, "The 'C' Should Stay in the YMCA," *The Wall Street Journal*, August 6, 2010, http://online.wsj.com/article/SB100014240527487 0427180457540549040545472.html.

3. "History: Sir George Williams," Westminster Abbey, www.westminsterabbey.org/our-history/people/george-williams.

4. "Dwight L. Moody: Revivalist with a Common Touch," Christian History, August 8, 2008, www.christianitytoday.com/ch/131christians/evangelists andapologists/moody.html?start=1.

5. Michael Parker, "Mobilizing a Generation for Missions," Christian History, August 6, 2009, www.christianitytoday.com/ch/bytopic/missions worldchristianity/mobilizinggenerations.html?start=1.

6. Mark Galli, "Missions and Ecumenism: John R. Mott," *Christianity Today*, January 1, 2000, www.christianitytoday.com/ch/2000/issue65/9.36. html.

7. John A. Murray, "The 'C' Should Stay in the YMCA."

8. Alec Hill, interview with Chris Horst, May 2013.

9. "Message From the Chancellor on Nondiscrimination," Vanderbilt University, Jan. 20, 2012, http://news.vanderbilt.edu/2012/01/chancellor -message-jan-20/.

10. Luke Hammill, "SA Senate Extends InterVarsity Christian Fellowship's Deadline," *The Spectrum*, February 26, 2012, www.ubspectrum.com/news/ sa-senate-extends-intervarsity-christian-fellowship-s-deadline-1.2797324#. Ugw3qG3OCJm.

11. Alec Hill, interview with Chris Horst, May 2013.

12. Simon Sinek, *Start With Why: How Great Leaders Inspire Everyone to Take Action* (New York: Penguin Group, 2011).

13. Simon Sinek, "How Great Leaders Inspire Action" TEDx Puget Sound, September 2009, www.ted.com/talks/simon_sinek_how_great_leaders_ inspire_action.html.

14. Ibid.

15. Ibid.

16. David Wills, personal interview with Peter Greer, July 2013.

17. Marty Caldwell interview with Peter Greer.

18. Dan Gilgoff, "Churches Fight Back Against Shrinking Membership," *U.S. News and World Report*, June 3, 2009, www.usnews.com/news/religion/ articles/2009/06/03/churches-fight-back-against-shrinking-membership.

19. Mathew Block, "ELCA Has Lost Half a Million Members," www.firstthings.com/blogs/firstthoughts/2013/06/04/elca-has-lost-half-a-million-members/.

20. Quoted in Dan Gilgoff, "Churches Fight Back Against Shrinking Membership."

21. Matthew 5:13–16 ESV

22. "William R. 'Bill' Bright, Founder of World's Largest Christian Ministry Dies," Bill Bright, July 19, 2003, http://billbright.ccci.org/public/.

23. Christina Ng, "Campus Crusade for Christ Changes Name, Losing 'Crusade' and 'Christ,'" *ABC News*, July 23, 2011, http://abcnews.go.com/US/campus-crusade-christ-losing-christ-crusade/story?id=14136976.

24. "Frequently Asked Questions," Cru, May 29,2012, www.cru.org/about-us/donor-relations/our-new-name/qanda.htm.

25. Louie Giglio, Cru, August 4, 2011, www.cru.org/about-us/donor-relations/our-new-name/louie-giglio.htm.

26. Andy Stanley, *Visioneering: God's Blueprint for Developing and Maintaining Personal Vision* (Colorado Springs: Multnomah, 1999), 158.

Chapter 7: Guardians of the Mission

1. Name changed.

2. Al Mueller, interview with Chris Horst, October 2012.

3. Lowell Haines, interview with Chris Horst, January 2013.

4. Suzanne Perry, "Obama Names Charities to Share His $1.4-Million Nobel Award," March 11, 2010, http://philanthropy.com/blogs/government-and-politics/obama-names-charities-to-share-his-14-million-nobel-award/21763.

5. Jon Krakauer, "Is it Time to Forgive Greg Mortenson?" *The Daily Beast*, April 8, 2013, www.thedailybeast.com/articles/2013/04/08/is-it-time-to-forgive-greg-mortenson.html.

6. "'Three Cups of Tea' Scandal Offers Lessons for Charities and Trustees," *The Chronicle of Philanthropy*, April 25, 2011, http://philanthropy.com/article/Three-Cups-of-Tea-Scandal/127251/.

7. Jon Krakauer, "Is it Time to Forgive Greg Mortenson?"

8. "ECFA Standard 2—Governance," ECFA, www.ecfa.org/Content/Comment2.

9. Terry Looper, interview with Peter Greer, February 2013.

10. Proverbs 28:23 ESV

11. Proverbs 27:6

12. Don Wolf, interview with Chris Horst, February 27, 2013.

13. John is a fictitious name.

14. Personal interview with Peter Greer.

15. Mark Taylor, interview with Chris Horst, April 2013.

16. Merv Auchtung, interview with Chris Horst, 2013.

17. Chris Crane, interview with Peter Greer, February 2013.

18. Tami Heim, "More on Leadership from Dr. Wess Stafford," Christian Leadership Alliance, April 3, 2013, http://blog.christianleadershipalliance. org/2013/04/03/more-on-leadership-from-dr-wess-stafford/.

19. "Primacy of Proclamation Board Resolution," Edify International, board meeting, August 2010.

20. "ECFA Standard 2—Governance," www.ecfa.org/Content/Comment2.

Chapter 8: True Leadership

1. J. Robert Clinton, "Three Articles About Finishing Well," 1999, http:// garyrohrmayer.typepad.com/files/3finishwellarticles.pdf.

2. Proverbs 4:23 NIV 1984

3. C.S. Lewis, *The Screwtape Letters* (New York: HarperCollins, 2001), 61.

4. Thomas A. Powell Sr., "Forced Terminations Among Clergy: Causes and Recovery," Liberty Baptist Theological Seminary, September 2008, http://digital commons.liberty.edu/cgi/viewcontent.cgi?article=1171&context=doctoral.

5. John 15:5

6. Psalm 127:1

7. Quoted in Fred Smith, "The Idol of Ambition," The Gathering: Fred's Blog, April 18, 2013, http://thegathering.com/blog.php?ac=post&id=180&p=1.

8. Fred Smith, "The Idol of Ambition."

9. Jim Collins, *How the Mighty Fall* (New York: HarperCollins, 2009), 27.

10. Thanks to Chris Chancey for introducing "humbition" to me.

11. Tim Stafford, "More Than Profit: A business plan with a divine edge has an angle on fighting poverty," *Christianity Today*, September, 18, 2009, www.christianitytoday.com/ct/2009/september/31.70.html.

12. Ruth Callanta, personal correspondence with Peter Greer.

13. John Piper, *The Roots of Endurance* (Wheaton, IL: Crossway, 2002), 160.

14. Harold Myra and Marshall Shelley, *The Leadership Secrets of Billy Graham* (Grand Rapids, MI: Zondervan, 2008), 53.

15. Ibid., 55.

16. Ibid.

17. Ibid.

18. Ibid., 57.

19. Ibid., 54.

20. Ibid., 57.

21. John 15:1–16

22. John 15:4–5

Chapter 9: Impressive Credentials Are Not Enough

1. "$43 Million in Debt, Big Idea Files Chapter 11; Assets for Auction October 28," *Reel Chicago*, October 2, 2003, www.reelchicago.com/article/43-million-debt-big-idea-files-brchapter-11-assets-auction-oct-28.

2. Phil Vischer, *Me, Myself, and Bob* (Nashville: Thomas Nelson, 2006), 223.

3. Marty Caldwell, interview with Peter Greer, January 2013.

4. Interview with Bruce Konold and Marty Caldwell.

5. Judges 2:7

6. Judges 2:10–12

7. Thanks to Paul Tripp for this example from his parenting videos.

8. Judges 2:15

9. Acts 13:22

10. 1 Kings 14:22

11. "Simply the Best," *The Economist*, April 13, 2013, www.economist.com/news/business-books-quarterly/21576071-lessons-leaders-simply-best.

12. John C. Horton, "3 Secrets for Improved Performance in Today's Economy," Collier Brown & Co., February 9, 2012, http://collierbrown.com/2012/02/09/3-secrets-for-improved-performance-in-todays-economy/.

13. Phil Smith, personal email correspondence with the authors.

14. Stephan Bauman, interview with Peter Greer, March 2013.

15. "Pre-Employment Inquiries and Religious Affiliation or Beliefs," U.S. Equal Employment Opportunity Commission, www.eeoc.gov/laws/practices/inquiries_religious.cfm.

16. Manya A. Brachear, "Help Wanted, but Only Christians Need Apply," *Chicago Tribune*, March 29, 2010, http://articles.chicagotribune.com/2010–03–29/news/ct-met-world-relief-20100531_1_refugee-resettlement-policy-hiring.

17. Jeff Johnsen, personal interview with Chris Horst, April 19, 2013.

18. Frank Lofaro, "Faith-Based Future," *Outcomes Magazine,* Christian Leadership Alliance, ym.christianleadershipalliance.org/?page=FathBased.

19. Danny Westneat, "Faith in World Vision Shaken," *The Seattle Times,* October 4, 2011, http://seattletimes.com/html/dannywestneat/2016405778_danny05.html.

20. Phil Smith, personal email correspondence with the authors.

21. Derek Bok, "The President's Report: Harvard University," 1986–87.

22. Mark Russell, "Character, Competency, Chemistry, and Chicken: An Interview with Dee Ann Turner, VP at Chick-fil-A," The High Calling, www.thehighcalling.org/work/character-competency-chemistry-chicken-interview-dee-ann-turner-vp-chick-fil#.UcShmfabhRE.

23. Stacy Windahl, "Young Life Lite," *Relationships Magazine,* Spring 2012, www.younglife.org/Publications/Relationships/2012/04/YoungLifeLite.htm.

24. Marty Caldwell, interview with Peter Greer, January 2013.

Chapter 10: Follow the Money

1. "Andrew Carnegie," Biography.com, www.biography.com/people/andrew-carnegie-9238756.

2. "Carnegie Millions for College Pension Fund," *The New York Times,* April 28, 1905, http://query.nytimes.com/gst/abstract.html?res=FA0F14FA355 913738DDDA10A94DC405B858CF1D3.

3. James Tunstead Burtchaell, *The Dying of the Light* (Grand Rapids, MI: William B. Eerdmans Publishing Company, 1998), 8.

4. Ibid., 40.

5. David Nasaw, *Andrew Carnegie* (New York: Penguin, 2007), 671.

6. Nico van der Merwe, *What Does God Know About Business? Making the Right Decisions in Tough Times* (Wapadrand, South Africa: Puisano Business Development Group, 2010), 40.

7. *Giving USA 2012: The Annual Report on Philanthropy for the Year 2011* (Chicago: Giving USA Foundation, 2012), 1, www.stanford.edu/group/scspi/_media/pdf/giving/galvin_givingusa_ar2012.pdf.

8. Ibid., 8.

9. Mark Crea, interview with Chris Horst, April 24, 2013.

10. Based on financial reporting contributed by International Justice Mission, Youth For Christ, Taylor University, and InterVarsity.

11. Bruce Konold, interview with Peter Greer, January 2013.

12. Roger Sandberg, interview with Peter Greer, April 25, 2013.

13. Ron Blue, "Wealth Transfer: Six Questions and Six Decisions," Generous Giving, http://library.generousgiving.org/articles/display.asp?id=142.

14. "CCMP Buys Generac Power for $1 Billion," *The New York Times*, September 15, 2006, http://dealbook.nytimes.com/2006/09/15/ccmp-buys-generac-power-for-1-billion/.

15. Kern Family Foundation, "About," www.kffdn.org/index.php/about.

16. Caitlin Gipson, "Leveraging Change," Azusa Pacific University, www.apu.edu/advancement/thanks/kern/

17. David Wills, personal interview with Peter Greer, July 2013.

18. Fred Smith, personal interview with Chris Horst, June 10, 2013.

19. Bryan Chrisman, personal interview with Chris Horst, November 2012.

20. Mark 12:41–44

21. Ron Blue, "Wealth Transfer: Six Questions and Six Decisions."

22. Proverbs 3:5–6

Chapter 11: Measuring What Matters

1. Amy Martinez, "Tale of Lost Diamond Adds Glitter to Nordstrom's Customer Service," *The Seattle Times,* May 11, 2011, http://seattletimes.com/html/businesstechnology/2015028167_nordstrom12.html.

2. Christian Conte, "Nordstrom Built on Customer Service," *Jacksonville Business Journal*, September 7, 2012, www.bizjournals.com/jacksonville/print-edition/2012/09/07/nordstrom-built-on-customer-service.html?page=all.

3. Jack McMillan, personal interview with Chris Horst, August 13, 2009.

4. "Best Companies: All-Stars," CNN Money, January 24, 2013, http://money.cnn.com/gallery/news/companies/2013/01/17/best-companies-all-stars.fortune/7.html.

5. Thanks to Brian Lewis for this analogy.

6. Dave Larson, personal interview with Peter Greer, July 2001.

7. Paul T. Penley, "Measuring Outcomes: Demonstrating the difference ministries make," Christian Leadership Alliance, Winter 2012 edition, http://ym.christianleadershipalliance.org/?MeasuringOutcomes.

8. Paul Penley, personal email with Chris Horst, April 2013.

9. Tim Skrivan, interview with Chris Horst, December 18, 2012.

10. Thanks to Tim Ogden for this important comment.

11. 1 Corinthians 3:6

12. Dallas Willard, "Living in the Vision of God," www.dwillard.org/articles/artview.asp?artID=96.

Chapter 12: Etched in Excellence

1. Name changed.

2. Elise Amyx, "The Christian Way to Land an Airplane," Institute for Faith, Work & Economics, May 10, 2013, http://blog.tifwe.org/the-christian-way-to-land-an-airplane/.

3. Colossians 3:23

4. History of the 99-Year-Old Buck Knife," *Popular Mechanics*, June 2001, http://wayback.archive.org/web/20070210073421/http://www.popular mechanics.com/outdoors/adventures/1277451.html.

5. Chuck Buck, phone interview with Chris Horst, November 7, 2012.

6. Matthew 5:16

7. "Statistics," Project 1.27, http://project127.com/about/statistics.php.

8. Derek Bok, "The President's Report: Harvard University," 1986–87.

9. Ibid.

10. Ibid.

11. Julie Y. Rhee, "Debauchery Comes Again," *The Harvard Crimson*, February 15, 2006, www.thecrimson.com/article/2006/2/15/debauchery-comes-again-debauchery-drew-sell-out/#.

12. "Harvard Students Celebrate 'Incest-Fest'," October 9, 2012, www.thecollegefix.com/post/11799/.

13. Marcella Bombardieri, "Harvard's Sexy H Bomb Magazine Drops," Boston.com, May 25, 2004, www.boston.com/news/local/massachusetts/articles/2004/05/25/harvards_sexy_h_bomb_magazine_drops/.

14. Colossians 3:23

Chapter 13: Culture Eats Strategy for Breakfast

1. J.R. Briggs, *The Towel*, www.youtube.com/watch?v=xzVcCDBwXJE.

2. Vistage team meeting with Peter Greer, April 2013.

3. James K. A. Smith, "Redeeming Ritual," *The Banner*, January 6, 2012, www.thebanner.org/features/2012/01/redeeming-ritual.

4. Miriam B. Weiner, "America's Meanest Airlines: 2013," *U.S. News and World Report*, April 08, 2013,http://travel.usnews.com/features/Americas_Meaneast_Airlines_2013/.

5. Karla Colonnieves, "How to Avoid Being a Do-Gooder Who Shows Up Late and Leaves Early," Fast. Forward. The End of Poverty, March 14, 2013, http://info.live58.org/blog/bid/239815/How-to-Avoid-Being-a-Do-Gooder-Who-Shows-Up-Late-and-Leaves-Early.

6. Shawn Parr, "Culture Eats Strategy for Lunch," *Fast Company*, www. fastcompany.com/1810674/culture-eats-strategy-lunch.

7. Andrew Ross Sorkin and Michael Barbaro, "American Apparel to be Sold to Investment Firm," *The New York Times,* December 18, 2006, www. nytimes.com/2006/12/18/business/18cnd-retail.html?adxnnl=1&adxnnlx= 1366690464–6IuiFE7k4OJXKlNppDk3Ig.

8. David Gardner, "American Apparel Founder Sued for $250 M for 'Turning Teenage Employee into Sex Slave,'" *Daily Mail*, March 9, 2011, www. dailymail.co.uk/news/article-1364324/American-Apparels-Dov-Charney-sued-250m-Irene-Morales-teen-sex-slave-case.html#ixzz2RFw0veyp.

9. Laura M. Holson, "He's Only Just Begun to Fight," *The New York Times,* April 13, 2011, www.nytimes.com/2011/04/14/fashion/14CHARNEY. html?pagewanted=all&_r=0.

10. Amelia Hill, "The Rise and Fall of American Apparel," *The Guardian*, August 25, 2010, www.guardian.co.uk/business/2010/aug/25/rise-fall-american-apparel.

11. Shawn Parr, "Culture Eats Strategy for Lunch."

Chapter 14: The Language of the Chameleon Club

1. Luke 12:8–9 ESV

2. John 5:1–15

3. John 11

4. Arnold L. Cook, *Historical Drift* (Camp Hill, PA: Wingspread Publishers, 2000), 61.

5. Deuteronomy 6:6–9

6. Elizabeth F. Loftus, "Make-Believe Memories," *American Psychologist*, November 2003, 867–868, http://faculty.washington.edu/eloftus/Articles/ AmerPsychAward+ArticlePDF03%20%282%29.pdf.

Chapter 15: Save the Church

1. Stephan Bauman, interview with Peter Greer, March 4, 2013.

2. Philip Byers, "About Dr. Ockenga: Unforgettable Name. Unforgettable Impact," *Taylor Magazine*, Winter 2009, www.taylor.edu/admissions/special-programs/honors-guild/about-dr.-ockenga.shtml.

3. Garth M. Rosell, *The Surprising Work of God: Harold John Ockenga, Billy Graham, and the Rebirth of Evangelicalism* (Grand Rapids, MI: Baker Academic, 2008), 216.

4. "History," World Relief, http://worldrelief.org/Page.aspx?pid=2687.

5. "Fact Sheet," World Relief, http://worldrelief.org/document.doc?id =1103.

6. "About World Relief," LinkedIn, www.linkedin.com/company/world -relief.

7. Stephan Bauman, Gordon College conference, June 2013.

8. David Bronkema, "Religion and the Politicization of Development," Chapter 4, "Missions Redefined and Politicized."

9. Name changed.

10. Gil Odendaal, interview with Peter Greer, March 2013.

11. John 3:29; 2 Corinthians 11:2; Ephesians 5:25–27; Revelation 19:7–9; 21:2, 9–11; 22:17

12. Gary Haugen makes a similar point in *Good News About Injustice* (Downers Grove, IL: InterVarsity, 2009), 212.

13. 1 Timothy 3:15 ESV

14. Beth DeGraff, "CRWRC Becomes 'World Renew,'" September 17, 2012, www.worldrenew.net/about-us/news-events/crwrc-becomes-world-renew.

15. Loving Our Global Neighbor Conference, Gordon College, June 2012.

16. Bryant Myers, *Walking with the Poor* (Maryknoll, NY: Orbis Books, 2011), 192.

17. "Millard Fuller: Habitat for Humanity International Founder," Habitat for Humanity, www.habitat.org/how/millard.aspx.

18. "Help Keep Habitat Christian, Founder Urges Baptists," *ABP News*, November 25, 2003. www.abpnews.com/archives/item/2658-help-keep-habitat-christian-founder-urges-baptists#.USRl_lqbgvg.

19. Ross Douthat, *Bad Religion: How We Became a Nation of Heretics* (New York: Free Press, 2012), 140.

20. 1 Corinthians 12:12

21. John 17:20–23

22. "The Future of Evangelicals: A Conversation with Pastor Rick Warren, Transcript," *Pew Research: Religion & Public Life Project*, November 13, 2009, www.pewforum.org/2009/11/13/the-future-of-evangelicals-a-conversation-with-pastor-rick-warren/.

Conclusion

1. Kelly Monroe, *Finding God at Harvard* (Grand Rapids, MI: Zondervan, 1996), 16.

2. Neil Swidey, "God on the Quad," *The Boston Globe*, November 30, 2003, www.boston.com/news/globe/magazine/articles/2003/11/30/god_on_the_quad/ .

3. Ari Goldman, *The Search for God at Harvard* (New York: Ballantine Books, 1992), 67.

Appendix 2: Primacy of Proclamation Board Resolution

1. Used with permission from Edify International.

Further Reading on the Topic of Mission Drift

1. Funding
   a. *To Sell Is Human: The Surprising Truth About Persuading, Convincing, and Influencing Others*, Daniel Pink
   b. *A Spirituality of Fundraising*, Henri Nouwen
   c. *What Does God Know About Business? Making the Right Decisions in Tough Times*, Nico van der Merwe
   d. *The Eight Principles of Sustainable Fundraising: Transforming Fundraising Anxiety into the Opportunity of a Lifetime*, Larry C. Johnson, CFRE
   e. National Christian Foundation, *www.nationalchristian. com*
   f. Generous Giving, *www.generousgiving.org*
   g. The Gathering, *www.thegathering.com*

2. Hiring, Training, and Culture
   a. *How to Hire A-Players: Finding the Top People for Your Team—Even If You Don't Have a Recruiting Department*, Eric Herrenkohl

    b. *Me, Myself, and Bob: A True Story About Dreams, God, and Talking Vegetables*, Phil Vischer

    c. *The Secret: What Great Leaders Know and Do*, Ken Blanchard and Mark Miller

    d. *Fundamentally Different: Building a Culture of Success Through Organizational Values*, David J. Friedman

    e. *Upended: How Following Jesus Remakes Your Words and World*, Jedd Medefind and Erik Lokkesmoe

    f. *Switch: How to Change Things When Change Is Hard*, Chip Heath and Dan Heath

3. **Metrics**

    a. *Reveal* study carried out by Engage International in partnership with Willow Creek Association, *www.engagechurches.com/reveal-about.aspx*

    b. "Does International Child Sponsorship Work? A Six-Country Study of Impacts on Adult Life Outcomes," *Journal of Political Economy*, Bruce Wydick, Paul Glewwe, Laine Rutledge, www.jstor.org/stable/10.1086/670138

4. **Board**

    a. *Leadership Is an Art*, Max DePree

    b. *The Fundraising Habits of Supremely Successful Boards: A 59-Minute Guide to Assuring Your Organization's Future*, Jerold Panas and Rich Devos

    c. *The Nonprofit Board Answer Book: A Practical Guide for Board Members and Chief Executives*, Board Source

    d. *Boards That Make a Difference: A New Design for Leadership in Nonprofit and Public Organizations*, John Carver

    e. *ECFA—Seven Standards of Responsible Stewardship*, *www.ecfa.org/content/standards*

5. Leadership

   a. *Leading With a Limp: Take Full Advantage of Your Most Powerful Weakness,* Dan B. Allender
   b. *In the Name of Jesus: Reflections on Christian Leadership,* Henri Nouwen
   c. *The Spiritual Danger of Doing Good,* Peter Greer
   d. *Lincoln on Leadership: Executive Strategies for Tough Times,* Donald T. Phillips
   e. *Virtuous Leadership: An Agenda for Personal Excellence,* Alexandre Harvard
   f. *Toward the Abundant Life: Transforming Lives, Transforming Communities,* Sylvia Palugod
   g. *The Roots of Endurance: Invincible Perseverance in the Lives of John Newton, Charles Simeon, and William Wilberforce,* John Piper
   h. *The Next Christians: Seven Ways You Can Live the Gospel and Restore the World,* Gabe Lyons
   i. *The Fabric of Faithfulness: Weaving Together Belief and Behavior,* Steven Garber
   j. *Humility: The Journey Toward Holiness,* Andrew Murray
   k. *Consequential Leadership: 15 Leaders Fighting for Our Cities, Our Poor, Our Youth and Our Culture,* Mac Pier
   l. *When Work and Family Collide: Keeping Your Job From Cheating Your Family,* Andy Stanley
   m. *The Monkey and the Fish: Liquid Leadership for a Third-Culture Church,* Dave Gibbons
   n. *Lead Like Jesus: Lessons for Everyone From the Greatest Leadership Role Model of All Time,* Ken Blanchard and Phil Hodges
   o. *The Conviction to Lead: 25 Principles for Leadership That Matters,* Al Mohler
   p. *Leading on Empty: Refilling Your Tank and Renewing Your Passion,* Wayne Cordeiro

6. General

    a. *Choosing the Good: Christian Ethics in a Complex World,* Dennis Hollinger

    b. *Wisdom & Wonder: Common Grace in Science and Art,* Abraham Kuyper

    c. *Culture Making: Recovering Our Creative Calling,* Andy Crouch

    d. *Bonhoeffer: Pastor, Martyr, Prophet, Spy,* Eric Metaxas

    e. *Kingdom Calling: Vocational Stewardship for the Common Good,* Amy L. Sherman

Peter Greer is a follower of Jesus, advocate for the poor, speaker, author, and president and CEO of HOPE International (HOPE), a global faith-based microenterprise development organization serving entrepreneurs throughout Africa, Asia, Latin America, and Eastern Europe. Peter and his wife, Laurel, have three children and live in Lancaster, Pennsylvania.

Peter is a graduate of Messiah College (BS, 1997), Harvard University's Kennedy School of Government (MPP, 2004), and Erskine College (honorary PhD, 2012).

Peter served as a microfinance adviser in Phnom Penh, Cambodia. He also served as a technical adviser for Self-Help Development Foundation (CARE Zimbabwe) in Bulawayo, Zimbabwe. In 1999, he became the managing director for URWEGO Community Bank in Kigali, Rwanda.

As an advocate for the church's role in missions and ending extreme poverty, Greer has been a featured speaker at leading conferences such as Harvard's International Development Conference, Catalyst, Urbana, Passion, and Jubilee.

Peter co-authored a faith-based book on microfinance, *The Poor Will Be Glad* (Zondervan, 2009) and co-authored a children's book on international adoption, *Mommy's Heart Went POP!* (Russell Media, 2012). He is also the author of *The Spiritual Danger of Doing Good* (Bethany House, 2013).

Follow Peter on Twitter: @peterkgreer or Facebook: @PeterKGreer.

To contact Peter for a speaking engagement, please visit www.peterkgreer.com.

Chris Horst is the director of development at HOPE International and manages a team of regional representatives located throughout the United States. Since 2006, he has served in a variety of roles at HOPE. As director of development, Chris employs his passion for advancing initiatives at the intersection of entrepreneurship and the Gospel to share HOPE's story with new and existing supporters. In addition to his role at HOPE, Chris serves on the boards of the Denver Institute for Faith & Work and the Colorado Microfinance Alliance. Chris has been published in *Christianity Today* several times. He received his BS in business from Taylor University in Indiana and his MBA at Bakke Graduate University. Chris and his wife, Alli, have one son, Desmond, and live in Denver, Colorado, where they are active members of City Church Denver.

Follow Chris on Twitter: @chrishorst.

Chris blogs at www.smorgasblurb.com.

Anna Haggard is the executive writing assistant at HOPE International, where she has collaborated with the president and the marketing department to write *Mission Drift* and *The Spiritual Danger of Doing Good*, contribute to *Transforming Microfinance: A Christian Approach*, and share HOPE's message through print and social media. Anna is a graduate of Asbury University and lives in Lancaster, Pennsylvania.

Follow Anna on Twitter: @annahaggard.

For additional resources, please visit www.missiondriftbook.com.

Also Available From Peter Greer

Charity and Service Have a Dark Side

From the front lines of service, Peter Greer shows how actions born from the noblest of intentions can become spiritually disastrous. His story is a compassionate warning for anyone who works in ministry or charitable nonprofits, from CEOs to weekend volunteers.

"Doing good can take its toll on our lives if we aren't careful. Here is an honest look at the dangers we all need to avoid as we seek to make a difference."
—*Craig Groeschel, senior pastor, LifeChurch.tv*

"In this extremely timely and important book, Greer applies the apostle Paul's teaching to the twenty-first century leader. Readable, humorous, and keenly insightful."
—*Brian Fikkert, author,* When Helping Hurts

"This book is a needed message for all leaders interested in social justice, ministry, or simply loving their neighbors as themselves. Read this book!"
—*Brad Lomenick, president and lead visionary, Catalyst*

The Spiritual Danger of Doing Good
by Peter Greer with Anna Haggard